What people are saying about …

Patched Together

"The simplest of stories often penetrate the heart most deeply … like this one!"

William Paul Young, best-selling author of *The Shack*

"For several years Brennan Manning has assured me in his writings that I am Abba's child, loved by God. *Patched Together* is no exception. Willie Juan's journey is Manning's, yours, and mine—broken human beings desperately suffering and in need of love. It is the story of God's journey too, He who comes down to take our suffering upon Himself, freely giving His love away. My soul felt restored while reading Manning's lifelong message in story form, and more, my heart ached in recognition of my own spiritual journey."

Lisa Samson, best-selling author of *Quaker Summer* and *The Church Ladies* and coauthor of *Justice in the Burbs*

"Brennan Manning's books have shaped the way an entire generation understands the love of God. I will never be the same because of them. In *Patched Together*, he carefully weaves words that penetrate your soul and change you from the inside. Thanks, Brennan; I love God even more because of your legacy."

Tom Davis, author of *Fields of the Fatherless* and *Scared*

"Brennan Manning is a master storyteller, and he has once again used his marvelous gift to remind us of the one story that bears repeating—because we need to hear that wondrous good news over and over, because we wander and forget, because our hearts are so easily hardened, and, most importantly, because it is true."

Ashley Cleveland, Grammy-winning gospel singer and songwriter

"Thank you, Brennan, for telling us your story again and again, only to remind us of the deepest story—that God is absolute Love and that there is truly and forever no catch! *Patched Together: A Story of My Story* tenderly reveals that God is the Grand Storywriter of our lives and He longs to write only Love on every piece of our stories."

Sharon Hersh, speaker and author of *Bravehearts: Unlocking the Courage to Love with Abandon* and the Hand-in-Hand Parenting series

"Absolutely beautiful. This is not Brennan's story alone. This is our story. We can find ourselves somewhere along its journey, where we've been or will be. And in the pages we see ourselves; we are consumed by the terrifying nearness and overwhelming reality of God's lavish love for us."

Candi Pearson-Shelton, singer, songwriter, and author of *Desperate Hope*

Praise for ...

the furious longing of God

"Sometimes I think that Brennan Manning's books should come with tear marks and nicotine stains. He dares to write who he is, and in so doing never fails to shape and change me into a more human, more honest disciple. *The Furious Longing of God* is one of the most startling apologetics for hope you will read this year."

Pete Greig, one of the founding leaders of The 24-7 Prayer Movement

the ragamuffin gospel

"In our society, we tend to swear unyielding allegiance to a rigid position, confusing that action with finding an authentic connection to a life-giving Spirit. We miss the gospel of Christ: the good news that, although the holy and all-powerful God knows we are dust, He still stoops to breathe into us the breath of life—to bring to our wounds the balm of acceptance and love. No other author has articulated this message more simply or beautifully than Brennan Manning."

Rich Mullins, songwriter and recording artist

"I found deep comfort in realizing that Jesus loves even me, a ragamuffin, just as I am and not as I should be; that He accepts me, though I am most unacceptable. I came to this book hungry; I tasted and saw afresh that our God truly is good and that He is, after all, for us."

Michael Card, musician, recording artist, and author of *A Violent Grace*

"So much religion is conveyed to us as bad news or bland news that we are immensely grateful when it is spoken freshly as good news. This is a zestful and accurate portrayal that tells us unmistakably that the gospel is good, dazzlingly good."

Eugene Peterson, author of *The Message*

"Brennan Manning does a masterful job of blowing the dust off of shop-worn theology and allowing God's grace to do what only God's grace can do—amaze."

Max Lucado, bestselling author of *No Wonder They Call Him the Savior* and *God Came Near*

"Some books are a great read. Some have taught me lifelong lessons that have made my life more of what I'm sure God intended it to be. And of course some have impressed my friends but gathered dust on my shelves. *The Ragamuffin Gospel* was and is different. It transformed me. I will never be the same."

Michael W. Smith, Michael W. Smith Productions

abba's child

"Brennan is my friend, walking ahead of me on the path toward home. As I watch him from behind, I am drawn to more closely follow on the path, to more deeply enjoy Abba's love."

Dr. Larry Crabb, author of *Inside Out* and *Finding God*

"Brennan awakens a sense of wonder at the possibility of real relationship with the Abba of Jesus. I was gently led closer to becoming a true child of Abba."

Michael Card, singer, songwriter, and author of
Immanuel: Reflections on the Life of Christ

"Brennan Manning has the wonderful gift of making Jesus a real answer to our real questions, a desirable lover for our ever desirous hearts. He does it again in *Abba's Child*."

Richard Rohr, founder of the New Jerusalem
Community in Cincinnati and the Center for
Action & Contemplation in Albuquerque

patched together

patched together

a story of my story

brennan manning
foreword by amy grant

David C Cook
transforming lives together

PATCHED TOGETHER
Published by David C. Cook
4050 Lee Vance View
Colorado Springs, CO 80918 U.S.A.

David C. Cook Distribution Canada
55 Woodslee Avenue, Paris, Ontario, Canada N3L 3E5

David C. Cook U.K., Kingsway Communications
Eastbourne, East Sussex BN23 6NT, England

David C. Cook and the graphic circle C logo
are registered trademarks of Cook Communications Ministries.

The Web site addresses recommended throughout this book are offered as a
resource to you. These Web sites are not intended in any way to be or imply an
endorsement on the part of David C. Cook, nor do we vouch for their content.

This story is a work of fiction. All characters and events are the product of the author's
imagination. Any resemblance to any person, living or dead, is coincidental.

Scripture quotations marked NASB are taken from the *New American Standard Bible*,
© Copyright 1960, 1995 by The Lockman Foundation. Used by permission.
Scripture quotations marked NJB are excerpted from the Jerusalem Bible,
copyright © 1985 by Darton, Longman & Todd Ltd. and Doubleday &
Co., a division of Bantam Doubleday Dell Publishing Group, Inc.

LCCN 2009941184
Hardcover ISBN 978-1-4347-0003-2
International Trade Paperback ISBN 978-1-4347-0047-6
eISBN 978-1-4347-0099-5

© 2010 Brennan Manning
Published in association with the literary agency Alive Communications, Inc.,
7680 Goddard St., Suite 200, Colorado Springs, CO 80920.

"Morning" previously published as *The Boy Who Cried Abba* by
HarperSanFrancisco in 1997 © Brennan Manning, ISBN 0060654562.

"Morning" and "Noon" previously published as *The Journey of
the Prodigal* by Crossroad in 2002 © Brennan Manning, ISBN 0824520149.

The Team: John Blase, Nicci Hubert, Jaci Schneider, and Karen Athen
Cover Design: Amy Kiechlin
Cover Photo: Getty Images, royalty-free

Printed in Canada

First Edition 2010

1 2 3 4 5 6 7 8 9 10

111609

I will open my mouth in a parable;
I will utter dark sayings of old.

Psalm 78:2 NASB

foreword

I was one of many listeners who first heard Brennan speak from a music-festival stage just outside of Boston. That was many, many summers ago. At the time he spoke of his conversion experience in a way I had never considered before.

Brennan's response to the love of God was so honest. He came up from his knees and ran outside under the stars, shaking his fist and screaming up toward heaven: "You are crazy … crazy to love me like that!" Brennan's passion, disbelief, amazement, confusion, joy, and gratefulness for the love of God and His gift of salvation released us all to experience again the wonder of being loved ourselves.

What a gift that was then. And now, many years later, with many miles travelled, many hands shaken, and many words spoken, he quietly pens this story. The retold story of Willie Juan. Brennan's story. Perhaps my story and yours.

I love a good story.

Patched Together transported me from the familiarity of my reading chair to the dusty landscape of Mexico and into the delicate heart of Willie Juan. Through his struggles and triumphs and heartache, we both continually rediscovered the love and mercy of God. I saw myself in Brennan's depiction of the scarred, ridiculed, cherished, gifted, redeemed Willie Juan. Life is unpredictable—sometimes beautiful and sometimes cruel. It seems we are all navigating the same road, running from and returning to the love for which we long.

Amy Grant

author's note

Dear Reader,

Patched Together is a very special story to me. It is, in many ways, my story.

You may have first read some of these lines in my two books—*The Boy Who Cried Abba* and *Journey of the Prodigal*. With the help of my good friend John Blase, I've taken those two books and revised and patched them together. Then I've sewn on a completely new patch in the form of a third chapter to complete the story. It's not seamless, but neither am I.

The book is divided into three sections: Morning, Noon, and Night. I've written this book in the Night of my life. Morning and Noon have passed; I've grown old and feeble and almost blind. For years now I've written about how much Abba loves ragamuffins. Sometimes, these days, I wrestle to believe what I wrote. Knowing that you're reading and wrestling along with me means more than you know.

I do believe that the night is always followed by morning. And that is when joy comes.

Under the mercy,

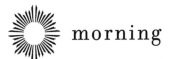 morning

"There is something more important
than understanding."

Willie Juan ran breathlessly through the streets of the village. Today was the day, the Fiesta of the Virgin of the Assumption, an occasion of great celebration in every Mexican town along the Rio Grande. Hopi may have been only a poor, rough-edged village clinging for survival to the banks of a very muddy river, but the people of Hopi loved their festivals. And the boy named Willie Juan may have loved them the most.

Once, long ago, Hopi was full of people. The prosperous silver- and lead-mining operations attracted visitors from near and far and supplied employment to most of those who lived there. But there was no desire to conserve, only consume. The ore was completely stripped from the earth, leaving little but dust. The mining operations took what they wanted and moved on. Many residents of Hopi followed. What remained could best be summed up in one word—*few.*

Willie Juan snaked through the village of small adobe huts, heading toward the heart of town. As he looked up, he could see the sharp peaks of the Sierra Padres rising in the west. Willie Juan assumed that there was something about mountains that didn't want to be plains. Brilliant whites and pinks and yellows stood out in contrast to the deeply shadowed granite of the mountains and the cloudless blue summer sky. The August sun made the colors shimmer and dance, as if anticipating the fiesta.

The Hopi that Willie Juan walked through had grown weary, its buildings groaning under the weight of time and the elements. The older adobe buildings had crumbled and melted away under the assault of wind and rain. Heaps of rocks on the surrounding hillsides masked the abandoned mines that once supported the community. Scrubby desert plants like *ocotillo* and prickly pear grew in spite of the harsh, dry conditions. The summer heat was brutal, over one hundred degrees today.

An adult would see and feel these things, but not a child. Willie Juan noticed neither the heat nor the decay; his mind was set on other things. He secretly hoped that today would be different, that today might be a day of belonging for him. He'd learned early in life that he didn't really fit in, he wasn't like the other boys and girls. He'd discovered that people, even kids, especially kids, can be cruel to those who are different. Most days at school the kids laughed at his odd-colored skin, tugged at his burnt-orange hair, and sometimes kicked his stiff leg. Willie Juan hoped today would not be like most days.

When he finally reached the center of the village, he quickly joined in the fun at the fiesta. His spirits were high. The fiesta was *the* highlight of summer—everyone in the village took time off work to celebrate.

Willie Juan bought himself a hot tamale and eagerly ran to join the games. He found a group of kids picking teams for tug-of-war. The thick rope stretched over a large puddle of water that the men of the village had made for the game using buckets and buckets of water. Willie Juan stood in front of the kids, begging to be picked. One boy shrugged and said *okay* and placed Willie Juan at the front of the line. But when the pulling started, his teammates suddenly let go. Willie Juan was jerked forward face-first and dragged though the thick brown mud. Like most days, the kids laughed and laughed as Willie Juan emerged from the mud and tried to wipe himself clean. They all thought it was quite funny, everyone, that is, except a little girl from the village named Ana. She was not like most kids.

Willie Juan walked away, away from the laughing. He didn't cry. *The boys were just joking*, he told himself. But why was he always the joke? He decided the kids wouldn't dampen his spirit; after all, this was a holiday. He spent a few minutes watching the parade and then wandered around the festive booths, smelling the glorious foods on the vendor's carts and eyeing many beautiful things for sale.

A little later he found his schoolmates pairing up for the wheelbarrow race. Most of the people in the village gathered to watch this particular race. The boys got to show off their strength and speed and make a plaything out of a work tool. The goal was to get across the finish line first with one boy pushing the wheelbarrow while his partner rode inside. Willie Juan hung back, trying not to think of the tug-of-war game. He watched quietly, as the padre organized nine pairs of boys along the starting line, each pair with a wooden wheelbarrow. At the end was a wheelbarrow with only one boy, Tino, left without a partner. The padre looked up to see Willie Juan standing off to the side by himself and called him over to be Tino's partner. Willie Juan was hesitant, but he trusted the padre. He hustled into the wheelbarrow, but when he looked over his shoulder, Tino's face was filled with anger; Tino was not happy to be paired up with one so strange, Willie Juan assumed. Still, Willie Juan turned back around, grabbed the sides of his wheelbarrow, and hung on tight as the race began amid shrieks and laughter.

Initially everything seemed fine, almost hopeful. Tino was pushing the wheelbarrow as if his life depended on it and Willie Juan thought they might actually win. The people cheered them on. But just before the finish line, Tino veered off the racecourse and dumped Willie Juan into a pile of brambles filled with black thorns. Once again, hope turned to laughter at his expense.

The boys guffawed as Tino turned and took a bow, obviously pleased with himself and the joke. Willie Juan crawled out of the brambles and slowly removed the thorns. He definitely hurt on the outside, but the deeper hurt was on the inside, where no one could see. Tino's little sister, Ana, walked by and glared at her brother: "Not funny, Tino." She smiled at Willie Juan, gently waved, then ran off with a group of other little girls.

Willie Juan just wanted to get lost, so he shuffled away into

a crowd of jugglers and musicians. One of the men was playing a soldier's march on a glistening, silver trumpet. Willie Juan
was amazed at the man's talent; he played with such ease. But
as beautiful as the music was, the thought he was left with was
"nothing will ever be that easy for me." Later, as the sun winked
good night, Willie Juan limped home to his grandmother, who
lived in a tiny house on the edge of the village. Sadly, Willie
Juan realized, this day had turned out like most days.

After Willie Juan arrived home, his grandmother plucked
out the stray thorns he couldn't reach, helped him bathe off the
last of the caked mud, and rubbed his scratched and aching
skin with aloe oil.

As his grandmother cared for him, Willie Juan thought
about how she had been considered "different" too. In her
youth, she had told him, she lived a very wild life, looking for
love in the wrong arms and for happiness in the wrong places.
But then, one day, a great change came upon her. She turned
from all she'd known, changed her name to Calm Sunset, and
retreated to live like a recluse in her tiny adobe hut. Visitors
were always welcome there, and even though she was very poor,
she loved having guests, and would offer a bite to eat, something to drink, and conversation.

"Grandmother," he said with a sigh, "why are the other kids so mean to me? I just don't understand. Why do I look so funny?"

Calm Sunset tugged him onto her soft lap and cradled him gently, telling him, as she had many times before, the now familiar story of his birth and the first few years of his life. She always called the story *Tuesday's child is full of grace* …

"It was a fine Tuesday in the village when you were born, Willie Juan. Everyone was curious about you, wondering …"

"What will he be? What will he be?" chimed Willie Juan.

"Yes, 'What will he be?' You see, your great-grandfather Jack had come to this country on a boat from Ireland, and your great-grandmother Lizzie was a former African slave. That meant that your grandpa John was African-Celtic, and he married your grandmother Mai, who was from Cambodia. So your father …"

"Johnny, right? My father's name was Johnny?"

"That's right, Johnny, was a mixture of Ireland, Africa, and Asia, and he married your mother, Consuela, who was from Mexico. Your mother was my daughter, and our ancestors include both Spanish and Indian blood.

"As a result of all this mixing, you have a very unusual skin

color, like no one had ever seen before. Your parents decided
on your name—"

"They named me Willie Juan. Tell me what it means,
Grandmother."

"Willie Juan, you tell me what it means."

"Willie from William meaning 'strong,' and Juan is a form
of John meaning 'beloved.'"

Calm Sunset smiled. "That's right. When you were just
a toddler, you and your parents were involved in a very serious automobile accident. Your right leg was crushed and some
burning debris from the car fell on your face and body, leaving burns all over your black, white, red, and gold skin. The
doctors did what they could for your leg and eventually your
burns healed, but there were many scars mottling your finely
burnished skin."

"But my hair wasn't touched was it?"

"No, Willie Juan. Strangely enough, your hair wasn't
touched—it has always been the same bright copper color."
Calm Sunset gently rocked him, stroking his head, ruffling his
hair.

"Your father was a migrant worker—he picked fruit and veg-
etables, following the sun and the seasons, traveling around the

country from field to field, picking the harvests as they matured. His job meant he was gone for long periods of time. Your mother stayed here to care for you. She herself took a job working in the fields of a local vegetable farm, planting, weeding, harvesting. Your father sent money and letters every week from strange, far-off places—Florida, Georgia, New Jersey, and Maine—and your mother would read them to you again and again. You loved your father very much and loved to hear his words as your mother read.

"Then, one day, the letters stopped coming. For many weeks the whole village held its breath along with your mother. We all felt that something must be very wrong. Finally, one afternoon, a worker who had traveled with your father returned home. He was very tired, but he made his way to your house to speak to your mother. 'I've news about your husband,' he said sadly. 'He's taken up with another woman, one with more money and a nice house. He will not be coming back to Hopi; we should not expect to hear from him ever again.'"

"Grandmother, did my father love me?"

"Yes, little one. I believe he did. Sometimes, Willie Juan, men get lost as years go by. That is, I believe, what happened to your father. It's very hard to understand." Calm Sunset paused. "Your mother was filled with a great sadness after your father left. She rarely smiled anymore. Without your father's income she was desperately short of money to care for you. She increased the hours she worked in the scorching heat of the vegetable fields. After many weeks of sixteen-hour days, she collapsed in the field one afternoon from too much sun. When they brought her to my home, she was dead. There may be only so much a human heart can take and then it breaks completely."

Willie Juan sat very quiet. The part of the story about his father always confused him, but the part about his mother made the sorrow come. Every time.

"If that would have been the end of the story, it would have been a catastrophe," Calm Sunset said. "But it wasn't. After her funeral I brought you here to live with me. My sweet Willie Juan, you have brought a joy to my days beyond what I ever imagined."

"So I'm not a cata ... catast ... what did you say?"

"Catastrophe. No, you are not, because that would mean your story had no brightness at all. But it does, Willie Juan. I like to say it's a tragedy; that means there is sorrow, but it's also mixed with moments of joy. Only God knows how much I love you, Willie Juan."

Calm Sunset had always lavished Willie Juan with warmth and tenderness; Willie Juan knew that she had done the best she could. But he could tell that she was now growing older, and she could not protect Willie Juan when he was away from her on the streets. Her love and care gave him a place of refuge at the end of the day, but it was no buffer against the world's laughter. And even though her aloe soothed the wounds she could see, he knew there was little she could do about the deeper hurts on the inside, close to Willie Juan's heart.

The night of the Fiesta of the Virgin of the Assumption, Willie Juan wept softly in his grandmother's arms. As his tears gradually gave way to sighs, she caressed him tenderly and whispered another story he'd heard so many times from her, about the Man of Sorrows. It was hearing of his love for her that caused her to stop running and change her name; such love, she had said, was simply stunning. But he loved all people, especially little children. Whenever children saw him, they flocked to him and never wanted to leave his side. *Let the little children come*, she whispered. *Let the little children come.* Long after Willie Juan had drifted off to sleep, she continued to rock him gently, whispering of the deep love of the Man of Sorrows.

The next day, Willie Juan woke up to a different kind of sadness. He was sad most days, but this didn't feel like most days. He was so unhappy about not having any friends that all he wanted to do was run and hide. As he stepped from his grandmother's house, he wondered where he could go to be completely alone, where no one could see him and laugh at him. A cool breeze blew against his skin and reminded him of the dimness of the adobe church in the center of the village, with its sweet fragrance of incense and mysterious peace. The church would be a place where he could hide.

Although he'd always been fascinated by the colors and images and music of the church, there was something that had always drawn him even more. It was the big crucifix over the main altar. However, he'd never dared go near. But this day, with a different, deeper sadness at his side, he decided to get a really close look. Sadness, pushed far enough, sometimes leads to a kind of courage.

Willie Juan stepped into the quiet church and slowly walked down the side aisle. Pleased that the sacred place was empty, he spied a stepladder in the sacristy and pulled it over to the main altar. Once it was secure, he climbed up for a closer look at the face of the crucifix.

Without hesitation Willie Juan reached out and gently touched the face, tracing the brow, the cheeks, the chin. Then Willie Juan looked up into the eyes. They were eyes like none he'd seen before: sad, gentle, and kind. As Willie Juan stared, he knew that this man on the crucifix was the great Man of Sorrows—the one Calm Sunset had whispered of many times, the friend of all children. Willie Juan continued to caress the face, recalling his grandmother's whispered words about this loving man, allowing the truth of his discovery to wash over him again and again. The longer he paused, the more he knew that this one loved him.

The man looked so thirsty and Willie Juan felt sorry for him. He scrambled down off the stepladder, got a cup of water, and gingerly climbed back up, trying not to spill it. Carefully he poured the cool water into the half-open mouth of the man. But the statue did not move its lips and the water ran down the painted chin, splashing onto the altar below. A few drops back-splashed onto the painted cheeks, making it look like his sad eyes had been crying.

Suddenly Willie Juan heard laughter's familiar scorn. He spun around quickly, nearly losing his balance, and saw three of his classmates. Willie Juan realized the boys must have crept in

through the side door of the church and witnessed his attempt
to comfort the Man of Sorrows. After jeering him, they ran to
the parish house and within minutes the priest returned to the
sanctuary with them.

"What in God's name are you doing?" the priest shouted.
"Never, never, never tamper with holy things!"

Willie Juan's classmates quickly ran out the side door, but
Willie Juan stood still, almost frozen by the priest's anger. "But
… but … padre, he looked so thirsty, and I just wanted to help
him …"

Willie Juan tried to explain about the man's sad, gentle,
piercing eyes, but the priest only scoffed at him. "It's a statue
and an expensive one at that!" he huffed. "Besides, only a priest
is allowed to handle these things; they are to remain untouched
by the world." With a captive, fearful audience of one, the
priest lectured Willie Juan about the *parousia* and about ascen-
sions and assumptions and eschatological realities and all the
other things he had mastered in his training.

When the padre was finished, Willie Juan mustered a
"thank you" and backed out the door of the church. The one
place he thought was a house of solace turned out to be just
another place of shame. He instinctively ran down by the edge

of the river; the gentle roll of the water over the rocks was comforting, like the feeling he'd had looking into the sad eyes of the Man of Sorrows.

The summer's heat finally surrendered as the cooling winds of autumn blew in over the mountains. Time passed for Willie Juan as it always had. But as the weeks went by, Willie Juan's thoughts returned again and again to the Man of Sorrows and his sad, gentle gaze. These thoughts always left Willie Juan filled with a myriad of emotions, from compassion to curiosity to wonder.

He was looking forward to the Fiesta of the Virgin of Guadalupe, the next big celebration in the village. Held in mid-December, the fiesta was a brilliant, joyful celebration. There would be fireworks, dancing, a costumed religious pageant, a jalapeña festival, and a torchlight procession that wound through the entire village. Best of all, there was a special carnival just for the children.

Willie Juan had been saving up money from his part-time job caring for the village donkey. Although it was a job no one else wanted, to Willie Juan it was a very important job. The village had one burro, Pedro, owned by Tino and Ana's father; it was stabled in the center of town. Until four years ago there had been running water, pushed to the huts by an electric pump running off the only generator in the village. But one night a howling thunderstorm silenced the generator. After that the water flowed no more. Now, because the village had no generator, it was necessary to travel with Pedro out to the *arriba*—the well in the desert—to carry back rations of water.

Each day after school, Willie Juan and Pedro would make the trip out to the *arriba* many times, bringing back loads of water for those who needed it. After he finished for the day, he would return to the stables, where Tino's little sister, Ana, who loved Pedro but was told not to get close to the animal, would hide in the stable until Willie Juan returned. Willie Juan then let her help feed Pedro and give him clean straw to lie down on. For his work Willie Juan earned six *pesetas* a week. Ana gladly helped for free.

By the time of the Fiesta of the Virgin of Guadalupe, Willie

Juan had saved up eighty-eight *pesetas*. With an additional twelve that Calm Sunset had given him, he set out for the celebration clutching one hundred *pesetas* to spend on anything he wished. As he limped eagerly into the village square, he marveled at the carousel's prancing ponies, the cotton-candy stand, the ladies in their brilliantly colored swirling skirts, the men in their sequined *sombreros* worn just once a year, and the colorful clown in a zebra suit dancing like a gazelle.

The crisp December air was filled with music and laughter and the mouthwatering smells of cooking food. There were old favorites like fajitas, burritos, hot tortillas, chili tacos, chilis rellenos, and nachos, and the special fiesta foods of enchiladas stuffed with chicken, pork stew with chilis and black beans, frijoles rancheros, green chili stew, savory corn bread, Raggedy Ann pudding, and sweet potato pie. Vendor after vendor lined the square, fires dancing merrily beneath the skillets, fragrant steam billowing into the air.

Willie Juan was lost in wonder. As he tried to decide whether he should buy a simple tortilla or a plump, juicy fajita, he caught sight of an old wooden wagon hitched to a small sorrel mare. On the side of the wagon hung a sign: THE GREAT MEDICINE SHOW. Curious, he headed over toward the wagon, pausing just at the edge of the crowd. Suddenly he felt his heart rise in his throat. A tall, gaunt, angular man stepped out of the buckboard and was about to speak when he locked eyes with Willie Juan from across the crowd. He stared at Willie Juan, as if he could see *into* Willie Juan. Willie Juan recognized the man, whose face was lined and worn with age. The eyes—there was something unmistakable about his eyes.

"The Man of Sorrows," Willie Juan gasped. He knew right away. The man smiled at Willie Juan, his face glowing like a sunburst after the rain, his eyes sparkling with joy. As the man approached, making his way through the crowd toward Willie Juan, Willie Juan found it impossible to move.

"Hello, Little Brother," he beamed. "I have been waiting for you. I hoped I would see you today."

Willie Juan was startled. He was not used to this sort of greeting. People were not usually pleased to see him.

"Won't you come and stand by me?" asked the man. He offered his scarred hand to Willie Juan. "Please, tell me your name."

"My name is Willie Juan," said the boy.

The man gently motioned to himself: "People call me Medicine Man. You seem very alone, Willie Juan." He turned and reached into the back of the wagon. "I have a special gift for you, Little Brother." He handed Willie Juan a small, clear bottle containing a bright orange ointment. "Rub three drops on your heart—one tonight, one tomorrow, and one the next day. Trust me, wonderful things will happen."

Willie Juan reached into his pocket for *pesetas*, but the Medicine Man waved him away, saying, "Keep your money, Willie Juan. What I have freely received, I freely give."

As the small crowd grew larger, the Medicine Man spoke to Willie Juan, but his voice was strong so that all heard his words. The Medicine Man said that the bottle held *amorine*—the Medicine of Love. He said it had miraculous healing powers—especially for heart trouble.

A voice in the crowd shouted: "That's all we need; a worn out old man selling love in a bottle. What else you got in the wagon—lamps with genies?" The crowd roared with delight.

"No lamps or genies," the Medicine Man answered softly. "Just love for free."

The crowd continued to laugh and mock, slowly drifting away, one by one. No one took a single bottle, even though the Medicine Man had continually offered to give it away. He finally sat down in the buckboard. Only Willie Juan remained.

Willie Juan approached him and shyly asked, "Señor, will the ama-amor-uh, the stuff in this bottle, will it make my crooked leg straight and make my scars go away?" Willie Juan was surprised by what happened next. The Medicine Man's eyes pooled with tears. Willie Juan was frightened. Had he said something to offend him? Was his question silly? Had the Medicine Man seen his skin up close, with all the scars, and regretted spending time with Willie Juan?

But the Medicine Man simply smiled and rubbed his eyes. "Yours is a childlike faith, Willie Juan ... of such is the kingdom. Yes, my medicine will straighten your crooked leg. As to the scars, don't be in a hurry to get rid of them; they are more beautiful than you'll ever know. You'll just have to trust me."

Willie Juan really didn't understand those words about the scars, but he did understand when the Medicine Man asked if he would like to share some lunch with him. Willie Juan couldn't believe it—sharing a meal was a sign of friendship. No one had ever invited Willie Juan to share a meal, not ever. In fact no one in his whole life—except his mother and Calm Sunset—had ever offered to share anything with him. Willie Juan began to feel things in his heart he didn't have words to describe; in fact his heart seemed even to beat differently.

Willie Juan was beside himself. He reached into his pocket, pulled out all his *pesetas*, and exclaimed, "I'll buy dessert—cotton candy, lemon ices, dandelion cookies—anything you want!"

They ate heartily; never was a meal so sweet. Willie Juan talked excitedly and the Medicine Man listened quietly. Willie Juan spoke about the deaths of his father and mother, the accident, his grandmother and her healing aloe oil, how hard school was, and how he wished for a friend, just one friend. He looked up into the Medicine Man's sad, gentle eyes and suddenly found courage enough to ask, "Señor … señor … would you … would you be my friend?"

"Yes, Willie Juan. I will be your friend," the Medicine Man quietly answered.

Willie Juan was thrilled. "I can't wait to tell my grandmother. As soon as I get home, I'm going to tell her that I have a new friend. She will be happy too."

They finished eating and began to clean up. As they gathered up the leftovers, Willie Juan noticed that there seemed to be just as much food left over as there was to begin with. "This is amazing!" he said. Willie Juan found a grocery bag to help carry the leftovers home. Calm Sunset would enjoy sharing the meal as well.

Then without warning, a cold chill gripped Willie Juan's heart. *I never had a friend before,* he realized. *And I don't know how friends act. The Medicine Man is so kind to me; he shares his food, he doesn't laugh at my scarred skin, he listens to me. What if I am not a good friend to him? What if I disappoint him? What if he changes his mind? I could lose my only friend.* Panic shook the whole of his small frame. Willie Juan grabbed the Medicine Man's hand and cried out, "Oh, señor, please tell me, what does it mean to be a friend?"

"Don't let your heart be troubled, Little Brother," replied the Medicine Man. "I'll share with you what friendship means to me—and by the way, it means a great deal. I'll tell you the kind of friend I am, and then you decide for yourself, Willie Juan, what kind of friend you want to be."

"Yes, señor."

"Little Brother, being a friend means loving completely. You don't have to understand completely, and chances are you never will. But that doesn't mean you can't love completely. That's what being a friend is all about. And it's really impossible to do that without the mercy of God. So you pray every day, 'Lord, have mercy.'"

Willie Juan, entranced by the Medicine Man's words, fell silent.

"Little Brother?"

Willie Juan was startled. "Uh, yes, señor?"

"Are you going to remember everything I've been telling you?"

"Oh no, señor—I mean, yes—I mean, uh …" Willie Juan was confused.

"Try not to forget," the Medicine Man said. "It's so important to remember."

Willie Juan had listened attentively, but he knew he still had much to learn about being a friend. He shook his head sadly. "Señor, to love completely … I could never be a friend like that. Besides, I'm just a little boy and I've never had a friend. I'm sure I'll just mess up."

"That's why I gave you the amorine, Willie Juan. It will help you to forgive and forget so that you can befriend yourself first; then and only then can you befriend others."

For some reason Willie Juan saw Ana's face. She seemed to like herself; maybe that was why she liked Willie Juan. Then his thoughts returned to himself. "So you're sure it will heal my leg and my scars?"

"Yes, my little friend. Just remember what I said about the scars, all right? They are beautiful if you learn to truly see." He paused. "And now, Willie Juan, I have to go. Good-bye. I need to go home to my father."

"Wha—what?" gasped Willie Juan. "Can I come with you?" The sudden announcement left him feeling abandoned, lonely, and afraid. In a pleading voice he asked again, "Señor, can I come with you?"

"No, not yet, Willie Juan. It's not time yet. There is a river that flows from the throne of my father. One day, far into the future, that river will call your name. Then you'll know it's time. You can join me then. Trust me."

Willie Juan couldn't help but notice that the Medicine Man used the word *throne*. He wondered if the man's father was a king. "Señor, who is your father?"

"I call him Abba."

That name sounded funny to Willie Juan, and he began to giggle. "Abba, Abba, Abba …" He let it roll around in his mouth, feeling how easy it was to say, how funny it sounded. It made his lips tingle when he said it quickly. Then he grew suddenly quiet. He was sorry he'd laughed. Maybe the Medicine Man wouldn't like people to laugh at his father's name. "I'm sorry, señor," Willie Juan pleaded. "I didn't mean to make fun of your father's name. Please don't be angry that I laughed."

"No, Little Brother," the Medicine Man responded. "My father is always pleased when you call his name, even when you play with it." At the mere mention of his father's name, the Medicine Man's face shone like sunbeams, and his eyes grew brilliant like starlight.

The Medicine Man stood and brushed tortilla crumbs off the legs of his pants. Willie Juan stood quietly and watched as the man began to pack up his buckboard and prepare to leave on his journey.

"Don't forget the amorine tonight, Little Brother. And by the way, thank you for the cup of water you gave me in the adobe church. I will never forget it. It will not go unrewarded."

Willie Juan couldn't believe his ears. What he did in the church was really good? "But ... but the priest said ..."

The Medicine Man gave Willie Juan a wink. "Oh, don't worry about him. This is about you." Then he climbed into the buckboard with a soft *cluck* to his horse and headed west, away from the fiesta and the little town of Hopi.

Willie Juan followed the buckboard all the way to the edge of town and watched as his new friend made his way toward home. Then Willie Juan made his way toward his own, running, skipping, jumping, and dancing all the way there. He sang, too, or at least he tried. It was just a few lines Ana had taught him while they fed the burro. He didn't know the name of the song, but the lines were full of joy, like he was:

> *"I've traveled far, the land and the sea.*
> *Beautiful places I happened to be ...*
> *Ave, ave, ave Mar-i-a ..."*

That night, Willie Juan couldn't stop talking. He excitedly told his grandmother about the fiesta—the parades and the lively music and the delicious foods. And he told her that he had found a new friend, although he didn't say too much about this friend. There was much about the day that was still almost unbelievable.

Willie Juan quickly ate his supper, kissed his grandmother good night, and went to his own little corner of the adobe hut, drawing the curtain across. He was eager to try the amorine. Wouldn't Grandmother be surprised when all his scars had disappeared and his leg was straight and whole! He knelt down beside his bed and pulled out the little clear bottle. He opened it slowly, then tipped it carefully to place a small drop onto his chest.

"Ow, that hurts!" he exclaimed in surprise as he felt the amorine begin to burn. At first the pain was skin deep, but then he began to feel it deeper, close to his heart. Willie Juan hadn't realized how deeply the boys and girls in his village had hurt him. But he continued to rub in the amorine anyway, because that's what the Medicine Man had told him to do. As he rubbed, he recalled the pain of being rejected, the humiliation of being ridiculed, the sorrow of being abandoned. The tears slowly welled and fell as Willie Juan cautiously began to forgive: his father, his schoolmates, the villagers, even his mother. At first the pain of forgiving nearly overwhelmed him; the memories of abandonment and rejection were so vivid, the hurt still so real, and the pain still so deep. But gradually, as he let go, Willie Juan began to feel the hurt recede, making room for other things, like peace, to flood into his heart. In the forgiving he was beginning to forget, just like the Medicine Man had said.

More than anything, Willie Juan wanted his leg to be healed, but the first drop had not affected his leg. So he decided to immediately apply the next drop. He started to open the bottle so he could pour out the second drop. Then, in the moonlight streaming through the window, Willie Juan looked down and caught sight of his scarred, disfigured torso. He moaned. The hideous scars glowed in the soft light, and he shuddered in disgust. He became furious. "I hate you!" he screamed at himself. "You're just a stupid mistake! Your scars are ugly! I hate you … I hate you!" He threw himself across his bed and curled up into a little ball, flinging the bottle away.

Even worse than seeing his own scarred body was the sudden anguish of betrayal. The Medicine Man had tricked him. He had applied the first drop of amorine, but Willie Juan's leg was not straight, his scars had not disappeared, his body was still broken and marred.

"I should never have trusted you, Medicine Man! You're

just what the people said—a worn-out old man selling lies in a bottle. You're a faker, a phony! You lied to me!" he cried. "I hate you!"

Feeling deceived, abandoned, and friendless once more, Willie Juan began to cry so hard that his whole body shook. Finally, physically spent and emotionally exhausted, he sank into a troubled sleep.

The next morning Willie Juan shuffled into the kitchen. Calm Sunset sat rocking gently in her chair. She looked at Willie Juan tenderly. "Come and sit by my side, precious child," she murmured. The boy nestled into the rocker beside his grandmother. "Tell me—why are you so sad?"

Willie Juan felt words flow from his mouth like a swollen river rolling over its banks, the words gushing in a torrent of pain. He spoke of the encounter with the Medicine Man at the fiesta, about having a friend for the first time, and about the man's father's name—*Abba*. He told Calm Sunset about the bottle of amorine, and last night's heart-wrenching failure with the first drop.

"Did you say *Abba*, Little One?" With her smiling eyes closed, Calm Sunset sat motionless for a long time. Then she placed her arm around Willie Juan's shoulders and said, "You are light to my fading eyes, Little One, and the love of my weary heart. How much do I love you? Only God knows how much. Let me ask you something. Do you know why the Medicine Man, when he was standing in front of the buckboard at the fiesta looking out at the whole crowd … do you know why he fixed his gaze on you?"

"No, Grandmother."

"It was because when he saw you, he saw himself, Willie Juan—the Man of Sorrows saw the boy of sorrows—wounded, outcast, lonely, and betrayed. In a single instant he understood you and read the sadness in your eyes. My little child, sometimes a sadness such as yours is the seed for the courage to be his friend. And your scars? Did he say anything about your scars?"

"He said they were beautiful, Grandmother."

"They hold a beauty this world knows not of, Willie Juan."

Relaxed in his grandmother's arms and soothed by her quiet words, Willie Juan was yawning, tired from his long, restless night. His grandmother didn't seem to notice.

Willie Juan curled up at her side. He wasn't asleep yet, but she must have thought he was. He heard her start chuckling—mostly to herself. "Ah, you silly old woman!" she whispered. "You bored the child to sleep! Perhaps you are not so wise after all. O Lord, have mercy on this addle-brained old woman. Show me, Abba, how best to help this little one."

When Willie Juan awoke a few hours later, Calm Sunset had fixed a breakfast of hot tortillas and beans for her grandson. During the meal Calm Sunset paused as if she heard something, or knew something.

"Willie Juan, listen carefully to me now," she said with quiet urgency. "You must leave here immediately and go to the Cave of Bright Darkness."

The boy's eyes grew wide. "Grandmother, why must I go there? Will you come with me?"

"I am too old to make the trip, Little One. And besides, this is a trip you can take only by yourself. When you reach the cave, you must stay there until one hour after sunset. Sit calmly and patiently. Listen to the silence. Watch for water, wind, and fire, and then wait for the storm to pass. It is not important that you understand everything I am saying. Remember, there is something more important than understanding. Do you know what this is, Willie Juan?"

"It's love, Grandmother, like you always tell me." Willie Juan remembered the Medicine Man's words about love and friendship. He still could not understand why the amorine had not healed his leg. It just felt like the Medicine Man had lied to him.

Calm Sunset helped Willie Juan pack a knapsack with a plump fajita left over from his lunch with the Medicine Man, a canteen of water, and a flashlight. At the last minute she remembered the amorine. "Quick, Little One, run and find your bottle of the Medicine of Love."

"Do you really believe in the medicine, Grandmother?"

"Yes, Little One. Trust me. Run and get it."

Willie Juan ran to the corner and dug around behind his bed to find the little bottle he'd flung away the night before. He shoved it into the pack; just seeing the bottle made him angry inside.

Calm Sunset helped Willie Juan slip his arms through the straps. "Now go, Willie Juan. All will be well." Her eyes glistened with love, and her voice rang with such authority that Willie Juan did not hesitate. She marked his forehead with the sign of the cross and hugged him tenderly. He departed at once.

With the knapsack strapped across his shoulders, Willie Juan scrambled across the slope that led to the steep ascent up the mountain. The Cave of Bright Darkness had been hollowed out of the face of the mountain by natural erosion and stood at an elevation of five thousand feet. Calm Sunset had once told Willie Juan that the cave had come by its name through more than three centuries of use by countless pilgrims as a place of spiritual retreat. Those who spoke of their experiences at the cave found them difficult to describe, using words like "luminous" and "shattering." Calm Sunset had gone on retreat there some sixty years earlier; she described it as the deep and dazzling darkness of sheer trust.

Willie Juan could never understand what the pilgrims were talking about. He only knew that the Cave of Bright Darkness was a holy place, perhaps as sacred as the church in the village. And now Willie Juan was becoming a pilgrim as well.

After hours of hiking, as the sun began its descent behind the far ridges of the Sierra Padres, Willie Juan pulled himself up onto the final rim. Before him a stone staircase wound down from the ridge to end on the ledge in front of the cave. Wearied by the long climb, his stiff leg throbbing with the effort, Willie Juan moved slowly down the twenty-eight steps, plopping down onto the parapet in front of the cave. He shrugged off his backpack, then reached for his canteen, tilted his head back, and drank deeply.

He looked out over the valley, realizing with some surprise that he'd never climbed this high before. His limp generally kept him down on the more gentle slopes near the village, except for one time that now came back to his memory. Last summer his classmate Antonio had dared him to climb to the narrow ridge. Willie Juan took the dare and began climbing. He was doing fine until he placed his good foot on a loose rock that rolled away and caused him to tumble down the slope. The jagged stones tore holes in his pants and made his knees and elbows fiery with pain. His hands were shredded by small cuts; wherever he touched his clothes, they left bloody smears. He remembered how hard it had been to see through his tears, and how Antonio had laughed and mocked him. He also remembered how Calm Sunset had patched his pants with quilt squares of brilliant reds and yellows; colors of love, no doubt, but also colors that drew the attention and jeers of Antonio and the other children.

As the painful memory passed, Willie Juan got to his feet and entered the cave.

Calm Sunset had told him the cave was always pleasantly cool inside, even on the hottest day in summer or the coldest day in winter. Willie Juan looked around the interior. A stone slab about halfway back into the cave looked like it served as a bed, with a few burlap bags that could be used as a mattress and blankets. In one corner there was a kerosene lamp, a rickety chair, and a battered oak table. An alcove in the other corner looked like a tiny chapel. It had a stone altar and a tiny tabernacle made of wrought iron interlaced with red velvet fabric. A tall crucifix stood behind the altar. Other than those items, the cave was bare.

Willie Juan limped toward the stone slab, climbed up on top, and wrapped two burlap sacks around himself. The strenuous climb had sapped all his strength. Within minutes he was sound asleep.

Not long after, he was startled awake by a deafening noise that sounded like the sharp report of a rifle. In fact it was a teeth-rattling peal of thunder accompanied by a howling wind and a relentless rain that slashed across the sky. Fascinated, Willie Juan slipped off the slab and stepped into the mouth of the cave. Suddenly a fierce bolt of lightning struck the shrubs and the wildflowers a hundred yards below, setting them ablaze.

The wild fury of the hurricane-force storm crashed against the mountainside in unabated intensity. Slack-jawed with wonder and sheltered by the cave, Willie Juan stared into the maelstrom. Transfixed by the cosmic spectacle, he was utterly unaware that he was unafraid.

Then, as if by a stern command from great authority, the storm abruptly ceased. Silence blanketed the Sierra Padres. So palpable was the quiet that Willie Juan felt himself becoming as silent as the valley before him, entering an interior place he had never visited before, a place of total inward stillness.

Out of the stillness came the whisper of a Voice: "Willie Juan."

Too startled to answer, Willie Juan looked around to see who was speaking.

"Willie Juan," came the whisper once again.

"Y-yes? I'm here. I'm Willie Juan. Who are you?"

"To most I am known as the Comforter, Willie Juan. However, they call me that for all the wrong reasons and are surprised when 'comfort' doesn't come. They have no tolerance for mystery, certain that they can know everything knowable. But I am beyond their knowing. I make my presence known in water, wind, fire, and whispers. I am without shape, form, or face. I am Spirit."

Willie Juan sat down and remained very still. Tilting his head, he listened carefully.

"You are brave, Willie Juan," the voice continued. "You have made a frightening journey alone to this secluded mountaintop. None of the other boys have done that. You are stronger than Antonio, who mocked you as you tumbled down the trail; braver than Tino, who dumped you into the brambles; more courageous than your weathervane friends who let go of the rope in the tug-of-war game. Your journey has begun in promise, Little Friend, but it could end in failure unless you are brave enough to risk the next step.

"You see, Willie Juan, the Evil One has studied you and discovered where you are most vulnerable. He has used your bad feelings about your leg and scars to tempt you to hate yourself; he is trying to steal the joy in your life. But this doesn't have to happen, if you can embrace what lies around the corner, even when it's unknown. It can be dangerous, because you will need to let go of your hold on life. You'll feel as if you're losing control, and the illusion of being in charge of your own future, of being the master of your own destiny, will vanish. For the first time in your life, you will understand just how much you are loved. It's risky, without doubt—but it will set you on the road to freedom. Do you have the courage, Little One?"

"Um, uh, what's around the corner?" Willie Juan asked timidly, clasping his hands tightly.

"Trust. Trust that everything that has happened to you has brought you to this moment—the car accident, your mother's death, your leg, even your scars. And trust that the good work that has been started within you will be brought to completion. But it's like stepping into the dark, Willie Juan. Are you ready?"

Willie Juan considered the voice's words. He could not understand everything he'd heard, but he remembered his grandmother's words: *There is something more important than understanding*. He knew that something was love; maybe love and trust were almost the same thing.

"Yes, I'm ready," he said. "I ... I am."

Then the voice said, "You have the heart of your grandmother, Willie Juan." And with those words the Spirit washed over him like the river traveling over the rocks outside the village, gentle but strong. The force was such that it knocked Willie Juan backward and the chair collapsed into pieces under him. Stunned, Willie Juan rolled off the broken scraps and started to get up, when he heard the voice again.

"Be still, Willie Juan, and listen closely. That rickety chair is like your old life of mistrust. It has just splintered into scraps," said the voice. "Now lie back on the ground and think about your grandmother. One whose love is even greater than hers desires to be with you."

With a ruthless trust that surprised him, Willie Juan lay back on the floor of the cave and remembered sacred times from the past with his grandmother—how proud of him she'd been when he returned from his first day at school ... how it had pained her when the other boys mistreated him ... how she would smile when he kissed her on the cheek ... how she had been kind to him when he grew sad and sulked, forgetting to do his chores around the house ... how her love never changed despite his funny looks or his sullenness or what he did. He remembered how Calm Sunset's eyes had glistened with love and confidence as he prepared to leave for the Cave of Bright Darkness. He didn't know many things; after all, he was only a boy, but this one thing he knew: His grandmother loved him.

Suddenly Willie Juan's reverie was interrupted by the sound

of footsteps on the stone stairwell. He looked up. A tall, gaunt figure filled the mouth of the cave.

"Normally it's my custom to stand at the door and knock," he said with a twinkle in his eye. "But since you don't have a door—may I come in?"

Willie Juan's eyes bulged, his mouth hung open, his heart raced.

"Medicine Man!" he gasped, jumping up and running to him. His feelings were all jumbled up inside his chest—the happiness of seeing his friend once again; the painful memories of giving up on the amorine and calling the Medicine Man a fake; fear that the Medicine Man would learn of his angry outburst and realize that Willie Juan had betrayed their friendship.

Barely able to breathe, Willie Juan stared at the Medicine Man's smiling face. His face looked more beautiful than a heaven full of stars and a radiant Hopi sunset and the glistening eyes of his grandmother all put together.

"You've been visited by the Comforter," said the Medicine Man. "He knows me in a way that no human being ever can. He taught you that unconditional trust is the seal of friendship. Trust is not out at the edges of friendship, but at its heart and center; you must learn to trust me unconditionally. Trust is the key that opens the door to love, Willie Juan."

The Medicine Man smiled but grew serious as he looked into Willie Juan's eyes. "I have come to find out how the drops of amorine are working. Tell me, what's been happening?"

Willie Juan felt all the blood rush from his face. "Yesterday I said some very bad things about you, señor. I didn't trust you. I called you a fake and a phony. I was so mad at you; I said I hated you." He lowered his eyes and wiped the tears that began to fall.

The Medicine Man took a couple of steps toward Willie Juan and waved away his concern. "Hush, hush, Little Friend. Would you believe I've been called much worse? Some of my old adversaries called me 'drunkard' and 'glutton.' Little Brother, you were forgiven before you asked. Now accept that forgiveness and be at peace. Don't punish yourself anymore.

"You know, there is an old saying that friends must eat a peck of salt together," he went on, "before they really know one another. They nicknamed my old friend Peter 'Rock,' yet he failed me in the time of testing. But, Willie Juan, it made our friendship stronger. Real love survives betrayal and deepens trust."

At that moment, forgiven and free, redeemed from the

corrosive power of mistrust, Willie Juan felt warm, as if he'd just been given the sun. All he could manage to say was "Want to split my fajita with me?"

The Medicine Man laughed and nodded.

Willie Juan ran over and snatched up his backpack. Digging for the fajita, he plopped down cross-legged on the floor next to the Medicine Man. He split the fajita carefully, handing half to the Medicine Man, who ate with great gusto. In fact the Medicine Man attacked the food with such single-minded relish, licking his fingers and smacking his lips, that Willie Juan watched in amazement.

Aware of his rapt attention, the Medicine Man said, "When you get to heaven, Little Friend, which is where I live, Abba will not ask you how many prayers you said or how many souls you saved. No, he'll ask, 'Did you enjoy the fajita?' He wants you to live with passion, in the beauty of the moment, accepting and enjoying his gifts."

Sipping from the canteen, Willie Juan looked into the man's sad, gentle, beautiful eyes and asked, "I know now you are the one my grandmother calls the great Man of Sorrows. But why didn't you come to the village with trumpets and angels? You came in a wagon."

"It's not my desire to frighten, Willie Juan. If I came displaying all of Abba's glory, you'd be afraid to come close to me and trust me, you couldn't bear it anyway. Besides, the amazing thing is not that Abba is big, but that Abba became small, like you, Willie Juan.

"Little Brother, it is my heart's deepest desire to be known, loved, and wanted as I really am. There are some people who have fashioned me in their own image and refer to me in grand language as the 'Supreme Being'—they much prefer those words to 'Man of Sorrows.' They really do not want to be associated with one who has been spit upon and ridiculed. They'd rather not follow one who eats with criminals and the outcasts. They view my scars as marks of shame rather than the witness of love. They are fair-weather friends; you have your share too, Willie Juan. They don't want the real me, but that's all I have to give."

Strangely comforted, Willie Juan reached deep in his pack for the bottle of amorine. He held it in his outstretched hand and asked, "Great Man of Sorrows, would you place the second drop on my heart? I'm not sure I can do it myself."

"No, I won't, Little Brother," answered the Medicine Man, and Willie Juan felt ashamed for asking. But the Medicine Man offered a compassionate smile that calmed Willie Juan's nerves. "I gave it to you because I know you can do it; it's a part of the trust the Spirit spoke to you about. It may surprise you, but I believe in you even more than you believe in me. You're one of a kind, Little Friend. You are beautiful because you reflect my beauty in a way the world has never seen before and will never see again." He paused for a moment. "Trust me, Willie Juan. I've provided you the amorine; now you can apply it. I believe in you."

With those words Willie Juan applied another drop of the medicine. As the drop began to be absorbed into his skin, Willie Juan experienced more room in his heart. He didn't understand how; he just knew there was. And it felt clean. Like love.

Willie Juan had been a little hesitant about getting too close to the Man of Sorrows. It was as if there were so many other things in the way. But now there was room. As he ran toward him, the Man of Sorrows opened wide his arms and welcomed Willie Juan into his embrace. His arms were strong and safe.

"Señor, please don't leave me. Please say you won't go. You said one time that my memory is not very good and maybe it isn't, but I do remember one thing you said to me that mattered the most: 'I love you, my friend.' Even if you were just kidding about my leg and my scars, I don't care. I'd be happy to stay just as I am, if only you would stay. Please don't go."

As he spoke, Willie Juan felt the amorine enter his heart, then turn and course back through his whole body. He knew that from that moment on, his life would never be the same.

Willie Juan hung on to the Medicine Man like his life depended on it; in a way he believed it did. The little boy's voice grew hoarse with deep affection. "I've never said this to anybody before—I love you, my friend. I really do."

With a sigh that seemed to rise up out of the depths of his heart, the Medicine Man said, "Willie Juan, don't worry. I will always be with you. I come in many different ways, but I'll always be there. Sometimes you'll see, sometimes you won't. But every time you pray, 'Abba, I belong to you,' I'll be in your heart praying to Abba with you.

"Oh, one more thing, Willie Juan," he added. "Before you run down the mountain to your house, go to the back of the cave and sit in the chapel for a moment. Trust me."

"I do, señor."

The Medicine Man embraced the little boy with great

affection, blessed him once more with his peace, and departed as suddenly as he had arrived.

Just as instructed, Willie Juan turned and moved back to the chapel. He walked into the quiet room, wondering how he could possibly experience anything more. He stood a moment, letting his eyes adjust to the subdued light, and then slid slowly to the floor. He looked up to the altar, lifting his eyes and raising his arms to the crucifix in thanksgiving—and could not believe his eyes. The torso of the crucified was tattooed with Willie Juan's scars. The face was streaked with tears. And the withered right leg of the crucified had torn away from the nail and hung limply in the air.

For the first time in his memory, Willie Juan stood on a straight right leg. And the scars? They were all gone, all except one on his chin. The little boy was amazed; the love of the Man of Sorrows was stronger than he ever imagined. He wept freely, softly crying "Abba, Abba, Abba." And as the tears ran down his face onto his shirt, they burned with a strangely pleasurable sensation. Willie Juan shuddered as a deep gladness welled up within him, gathering such warmth and force that it seemed his chest would surely burst. As he opened his mouth, the joy became the simple lines of the song Ana had taught him:

"Ave, ave, ave Ma-ri-a,
Ave, ave, ave Mari-a ..."

Willie Juan had no time to feel the sadness of good-bye. He hurriedly picked up his backpack, canteen, and flashlight and began his scramble down the mountain. An hour later, flashlight in hand, he reached home whispering, "Abba, I belong to you," and rushed into the arms of his grandmother. In no time, Willie Juan was fast asleep.

By the following morning, word had spread through the entire village of Hopi that little Willie Juan had made the dangerous journey to the Cave of Bright Darkness all alone. Many people gathered in front of his house. The padre pushed his way through the crowd, entered the house, and confronted Calm Sunset: "Good heavens!" he said. "What happened to Willie Juan's leg and scars? I don't understand."

Calm Sunset looked at Willie Juan and winked. "There is something more important than understanding, padre."

"Well, I'm not sure what that would be."

Willie Juan stood tall on his straight right leg and rubbed the scar on his chin. "I know, padre. Trust me."

noon

*"Try not to forget," the Medicine Man
said. "It's so important to remember."*

One of the hindrances to the spiritual life is amnesia. Just such a thing happened to Willie Juan as the years went by. The village of Hopi forgot about the miracles in Willie Juan's life too. It wasn't intentional necessarily; there were just other matters that took precedence in the village's memory. The children around him grew and their lives changed: Tino, Ana, and the others. The village's water pump was repaired, so there was no longer any need for Willie Juan and Ana to feed and water Pedro. The experiences with the Man of Sorrows and the Cave of Great Darkness waned in Willie Juan's mind. Oh, he remembered them, but life crowded them, diluted them somewhat.

He went through grade school without distinction. His marks were very ordinary. Though he studied hard, he just couldn't seem to remember what he read, especially the long answers in his religion classes. He tried sports but wasn't coordinated; the years of walking on a lame leg had caused his balance to be off, even after his leg was healed. He auditioned for the school's small orchestra, hoping to play the trumpet, but the director said, "Not everyone was meant to play." He even failed as an altar boy because he rang the bell when he should have brought the book, and he had a tendency to shout "Alleluia" anytime it seemed like the right thing to do. To cap it all off, one day his eyes started watering and they seemed to grow worse with each passing day.

So one of the best parts of every day for Willie Juan was when the final school bell of the afternoon rang. He was always ready and waiting to be freed to do what he wanted to do. And he could always be found outside his grandmother's house, whittling with his penknife. The knife had been his father's; Calm Sunset gave it to him one year as a birthday present. Willie Juan couldn't do much with books and pencils, but he discovered that he had a special talent for wood carving. An ugly stick or a block of wood took shape, contour, and form under the magic of the blade in his long, sinewy hands.

The neighbors often marveled at his ability. In their amnesia for Willie Juan's miraculous past, the town members didn't expect anything like this from him.

But his grandmother never forgot. She praised Willie Juan for his talent, but never acted surprised by it. In time, with Calm Sunset's encouragement, Willie Juan went to a vocational school to study woodcrafting. Soon enough Willie Juan noticed that even his teacher began to learn from him.

Once he worked for three weeks, carving a dead piece of wood as a gift for his grandmother. He had whittled the face of the great Man of Sorrows. When he presented it to her, she stared in amazement, her eyes filled with tears.

"Willie Juan," she said, "he almost seems alive."

"He is, Grandmother."

"Why is he smiling?" she asked.

"Just because he is the Man of Sorrows doesn't mean he's always sad," Willie Juan said. "He grins a lot and his eyes twinkle. Sometimes he throws back his head and he laughs and laughs, and he makes me laugh too. At least as best as I can remember."

Money for life's necessities was scarce in Hopi. Eventually there was none at all. Heavy rains destroyed the soybean crops and unemployment was rampant. Upon graduation from wood-crafting school, though his grandmother fussed a little, Willie Juan told her that he had to leave town to find work, but would come back in a few months with money.

He traveled across the Laredo River under cover of darkness, eluded the border patrol, and made his way to the house of a Hopi migrant worker who was now living in the big city. The migrant workers welcomed him and got him a menial job in the barrio.

Willie Juan continued his wood carving, and as in Hopi he quickly attracted attention. A merchant volunteered to sell Willie Juan's pieces in his store. One day a wealthy tourist spotted a carving of a small lamb. "Amazing!" he cried. "Who is the artist?"

Willie Juan suddenly found himself transported to Santa Fe, New Mexico, staying in a mansion and commissioned to carve a bust of José Antonio Luis, an aesthetic millionaire and patron of the arts. One afternoon, at a lavish garden party for Santa Fe's aristocracy, the bust was unveiled. The crowd was speechless. Finally someone gasped, "Miraculous! Stunning! Lifelike resemblance! Who is the artist?"

Soon commissions rolled in for Willie Juan, along with thousands and thousands of dollars. He bought a home in Santa Fe and arranged for his grandmother to visit often. He became friends with his neighbors and was a regular presence at the cathedral. He also began seeing an eye doctor regularly; his watering eyes were only growing worse.

At Mass one Sunday, the priest talked about God's love for *los pobres*—the poor. He stressed the need for those with much to give much. Willie Juan was so moved by the message that he left church and went directly to the barrio intent on giving away a lot of money. He stopped at a corner where he saw a young girl selling fruit and candy. As he approached, he heard her humming a tune that felt very familiar. But the tune was quickly overshadowed by her physical presence. Willie Juan could only stand and stare. She was thin, wore a simple dress, and had skin that glistened like honey. But the feature that completely captured Willie Juan was her face. Her eyes were of the deepest brown; her nose was sculpted; her smile and countenance were radiantly beautiful.

Just then a fat Anglo customer with a ruby in his right ear and a fifty-dollar bill in his hand approached and said to the girl, "Whisper something dirty in my ear and this fifty is yours."

She lowered her eyes and said softly, "No, sir, I would never do that."

The man snorted, screamed obscenities at her, and stormed off.

"Beautiful!" Willie Juan whispered to himself, deeply moved by an innocence he thought no longer existed. He found the courage to speak to her and hoped the words would follow. Not three steps away from her, she turned to face the other direction and began humming once more. "Excuse me, but may I ask you your name?" The girl turned and found Willie Juan's eyes. And her smile followed.

"Willie Juan?"

And suddenly Willie Juan was able to put the tune and the face to a name. "Ana?"

"Yes, it's me."

Willie Juan was beside himself. "What are you doing here, Ana?"

The next few moments were full of compressed time. Ana explained that after her mother died, Ana, Tino, and her father had moved around many places since their days in Hopi. Her father had worked close to Santa Fe for a while and they had lived with one of his sisters. But her father had become sick and died quickly. Tino moved back to Hopi, but she stayed put.

Willie Juan bought all the fruit and candy she was selling and asked if he might walk her home. "Yes, you may. It's not far." When they arrived at her home, Willie Juan couldn't believe the grinding poverty and heartrending squalor. The little cardboard shack she called home was barely eight feet long, yet it was brightly colored and spotlessly clean. It was occupied by several little children who seemed to have nowhere else to go.

Willie Juan was moved by Ana—she was something more than "pretty," for he had seen pretty girls before and they didn't glow like she did. The only word that seemed to fit his childhood friend was, again, *beautiful*, because pure beauty seemed to radiate from her soul. It entered his open heart and warmed him from the inside out.

Willie Juan thought, *I am in love*. He remembered those childhood afternoons when he let Ana help him feed Pedro the burro. He had always really enjoyed those moments; they were happy memories. He was beginning now to see that Ana had been a friend to him when no one else had. A beautiful friend.

On their second date Willie Juan invited Ana to his house for a luxurious afternoon visit, but she refused. He could not understand why anyone would turn down such comfort. *Perhaps it's too soon,* he thought. *When she knows me better, she will agree to visit my home.*

Ana and Willie Juan saw each other every day for weeks. Each afternoon he bought the fruit and candies Ana had to sell so he could take her away from the streets for a while. They took long walks and would sit by the river. Willie Juan always had a piece of wood in his hands, gradually carving an image of Ana's radiant face. Ana had told Willie Juan that she was impressed by his talent, but more by the fact that he seemed to really see her.

Every evening she asked him to walk her back to her makeshift home in the barrio so she could look after all the children who would wander in at dusk. They were orphaned or abandoned, and always welcome. Ana made room for as many as would come; she fed them whatever she could, never turning any away. As the children ate, Ana would set to work patching torn clothes or mending socks with holes. There were some holes Ana just could not patch, but that didn't keep her from trying. Willie Juan was astounded by Ana's generosity—her giving spirit reminded him of his grandmother.

On the way back to her home each evening, they would stop in the marketplace, and Willie Juan would buy more food for the evening than Ana could have bought in an entire month. Together they'd carry it back to Ana's and then the older children would help her prepare the evening meal for all of them, all except Willie Juan. He always left after helping to carry in the baskets of food. He just couldn't bring himself to stay in that wretched place any longer than he had to. And it broke his heart to see Ana living there. He just could not understand. Willie Juan vowed to himself, "One day I will take Ana away from this poverty."

He told his grandmother about his relationship with Ana, and she was thrilled. "You never knew it, Willie Juan, but she was taken with you as a boy. You don't really think she liked Pedro the burro that much, do you?"

"I don't know," he replied, grinning slightly. "Pedro was a little smelly." They both laughed.

"Please bring her to see me someday."

"*Sí*, Grandmother."

The following night, Willie Juan walked hand in hand with Ana along the riverbank. As they walked, she told him that she admired his gentle, honest, and uncomplicated ways. Humbled by her tenderness, Willie Juan realized by the way that she looked at him that his grandmother was right: She was, and always had been, taken with him. Suddenly Willie Juan stopped: "Ana, I love you with all my heart, and I am asking you to marry me. I will take you away from the barrio to live in my spacious house high on the hill, with running water and a flower garden and a bathtub."

"Oh, Willie Juanito," she said, using her pet name for him. "I love you too, and I am so honored that you want me to be yours. But I could never leave the barrio. My heart is with my people."

Willie Juan's jaw dropped. "What? I don't understand. You mean to marry you I must live like you in a little cardboard shack with no water and no bathtub? I have worked so hard to get away from all that."

Her eyes said it all. "I am sorry, Willie Juanito. I know you don't understand, but maybe you don't have to understand to love me?" Willie Juan knew he had heard something like that many years ago, but he couldn't remember who said it. Willie Juan went home that night torn up inside and made a vow. "If Ana won't come with me, then I'll never go back there. Never."

Constantly clutching his half-completed wood carving of Ana, Willie Juan moped around his house for weeks. His vision was getting worse, but he thought it was because he had cried so much. His grandmother tried to comfort him, but nothing she said or did could help.

Then one evening there was a knock at the door. It was Ana's aunt, Isabel. She told Willie Juan that Ana had been struck and killed by a car. Ana was dead by the time the ambulance arrived.

Willie Juan sank to the floor as his legs gave way beneath him. He was enraged. He cried out, "Abba, where were you? Why didn't you protect Ana? Why?"

Grief-stricken, he dragged himself to the funeral Mass and out to the cemetery. A gentle rain was falling. His sight was deteriorating rapidly. So the priest read him the inscription on her tombstone. "Here lies Ana Wim, God's little one."

"Ana Wim? Ana's last name was Gonzales. I don't understand." Willie Juan was quite confused.

"We all knew her as Ana Wim. It was the name she lived by here."

When the priest explained the tradition in the Bible of the "Anawim," the long line of Israel's little ones who loved the poor and being poor and had unfailing trust in God, Willie Juan was racked with guilt and even more grief. At home he was inconsolable.

Unfortunately his grandmother had to leave suddenly for Hopi because her best friend was quite sick. Willie Juan knew that his grandmother was doing the right thing. And besides, he thought, it didn't really matter whether she was home with him or not. Her attempts to comfort him were appreciated, but powerless against the weight of death.

To add to it all, he could hardly see now. When he held the wood carving of Ana's face in his hands, he had to see it in his mind's eye. Where once was emerging beauty, now he only saw a blur. First he lost his beloved Ana, and now his sight.

Alone and lonely, his heart ready to break with sorrow, Willie Juan stumbled through the house bumping into chairs and tables. Two weeks after Ana's death, he went totally blind. The doctors used big words like "progressive deterioration of the retina." To Willie Juan he had been forsaken.

Since arriving in Santa Fe, Willie Juan's memory of the Medicine Man had been steadily fading into the distance, long before his sight began to fade. He'd been caught up in career, romance, recognition, prosperity, and taking a hot bath every day; an awareness of Abba and the Man of Sorrows was simply crowded out. Now, with those things taken away, he had the time for Abba, but not the desire. He grew demanding: "Where were you when that driver struck down my Ana? Where were you? And where are you now that my eyesight is gone? You told me long ago that you were my friend. I thought I was yours. It must have all been a lie."

Asking but getting no answers, he turned to tequila. The drink dulled the pain; it did not take it away, but at least it wasn't as piercing. He stumbled around the house with his cane, drunk most of the time, refusing to answer the door or the telephone. His guilt and shame over Ana, about preferring comfort and nice things to her love, was almost more than he could bear. How could he have been so blind?

When he chose not to marry and live with Ana, he hadn't considered the words from the Man of Sorrows, about how, with God's mercy, it is possible to love completely without understanding completely. Those words could have shed light on Willie Juan's darkness, too, but he remembered none of them now.

Depression followed the euphoria of tequila. Willie Juan at first believed the darkness could grow no darker. But he was wrong. In the black of total blindness, on one evening when the well of depression was deeper and darker than ever, Willie Juan quite possibly made his most dangerous vow: "I will never care again."

Early one morning Ana's aunt Isabel knocked on Willie Juan's door. Willie Juan pretended to still be asleep. Isabel knocked once more and then a few moments later Willie Juan heard her yell from outside his window: "Willie Juan, I have something for you."

Isabel's announcement was enough to pique Willie Juan's curiosity. He had not seen her since the funeral. Willie Juan stumbled through the house to the front door, yelling, "What is it?" He repeated the question as he cracked open the front door.

Isabel stood with a package in her arms. "It is something for you ... from Ana. We found it among her things. There was a card attached that had your name on it." Isabel unwrapped the package. She placed it in Willie Juan's hands; he felt the valves, slides, and the bell of a trumpet.

"Wh—?" and then memory flooded Willie Juan's mind. One evening as they sat and talked by the river, Ana had asked what one thing he wished he could do. He told her about a man who had visited Hopi, a traveling musician. He dazzled everyone with his trumpet playing. "I would like to be able to do what he did," Willie Juan said.

"You'll never learn to play the trumpet while drowning

your pain in tequila, Willie Juan; the only thing you're drowning is yourself. Ana would not want this for you. Maybe this trumpet is something you need right now. Maybe you can give your pain a song. She loved you completely," said Isabel. "Now go back to sleep."

Hours later Willie Juan awakened with his head pounding and his heart aching. He reached for the tequila but his hands found the trumpet. The musician in Hopi had shown Willie Juan how to hold a trumpet, even how to blow through the mouthpiece. But that was long ago.

Still quite fuzzy, he said to himself, "I will try this, once, for Ana." He raised the trumpet to his pursed lips and blew. He filled the instrument with the pain in his heart and it emerged from the trumpet as melody. Willie Juan was amazed. He couldn't sing, he had no musical training, but the instant the trumpet reached Willie Juan's mouth, beautiful music emerged. At that moment it became a symbol of trust to Willie Juan, something he had lost somewhere along the way.

Pouring out his agony into the trumpet, he unleashed torrents of sixteenth notes at blinding speed, then throttled down wistfully into the middle register of the horn in a wailing cry. He had once heard a poet say, "Whatever is not written will be wept." With his trumpet Willie Juan was writing his heart's lament. He hadn't experienced something this miraculous since that day in the Cave of Bright Darkness. But that was long ago.

"Magic, sheer magic!" cried a neighbor down the street, who owned the Repertory Theater and had heard him playing. "You must share this gift with the people of Santa Fe. Clean yourself up. You'll open next week's performance." And that was that.

The next week Willie Juan's grandmother returned from Hopi and attended the theater with him. Willie Juan opened with a five-man ensemble. He stood in the middle of the stage, his feet planted firmly on the ground, his slender frame shivering. Willie Juan was to begin with a solo. The sounds that came screaming out of the trumpet in driving, pulsing, melodic thrusts were intensely personal notes of Willie Juan's grief. The five-man ensemble lowered their instruments and Willie Juan heard them back away slowly. The grief he played, while quite personal, was also general, he noticed. Everyone there had felt it sometime, somehow.

The following morning Calm Sunset read Willie Juan the

reviews. The music critic of a prestigious local newspaper wrote, "Last night a skinny, blind man ambled onto the stage, hiked up his horn, and blew the roof off the Repertory Theater. In one dazzling performance he did everything that has ever been done with a trumpet. This guy is going places."

And he did. Yet although he forgot much about the past, he remembered Hopi. As his wealth increased, he was faithful to anonymously send large gifts to the mayor of the village, encouraging him to use the money to revive the town.

Willie Juan rose to meteoric superstardom, far beyond his modest wood-carving fame. He soon found himself on the top stages around the world playing to packed houses. His stunning arrangements introduced a new era both to classical and jazz concerts. His harmonies and rhythms grew more complex, and his swiftly changing chords and furious tempos required an astonishing command of the instrument. But even still, the fuel for it all was his pain.

After two years of touring the country and the world, his hour of triumph arrived: a trumpet concert with the full philharmonic orchestra in New York City.

Later that week the *New York Times* reported:

> A ragamuffin blind man named
> Willie Juan brought the trum-
> pet to a place that it has never
> been before. His glowing, rounded
> tones, technical precision, and
> fully developed sense of flow
> and shading were spellbinding. He
> swooped and slid through the full
> range of the horn. In the finale,
> when he flirted outrageously with
> the melody, climbing in counter-
> point, tossing notes and nuances
> back and forth in the air, the
> heavens fell silent and Gabriel
> envied. He may not be able to see,
> but we can—the man with the horn
> owns the City.

Every other major magazine and newspaper confirmed these facts; all that is, except one. Sometimes the facts have little to do with the truth. A small, independent reviewer said:

> Willie Juan's self-absorption and
> aloofness reveal a brokenness that
> needs mending. No one can deny
> his miraculous gift, but one won-
> ders what vows were made along the
> way …

It just takes one brave voice to tell the truth.

Willie Juan felt the words beneath his skin. His heart was empty, and that made his triumph trivial. He canceled his upcoming world tour and withdrew. Once again he became a solitary man. He lay awake night after night. He knew his music had fire, soul, and blues; what it didn't have was joy.

Willing Juan felt like a walking shell that was once filled with personality. He still used his cane, and all of his gestures moved and seemed human, but some fire inside had died. He had lost what a beloved poet called "the inward music." He was a sad, blind, wood carver and trumpeter who could hit the notes, but was missing the song. He had played all the grief he could find within. But now there was nothing.

He was uneasy and restless. One night, in his tossing and turning, he heard church bells—the *Ave*. He had stopped attending church after Ana's death, but when the bells rang that morning, they reminded him of her song: "Ave, ave, ave Mari-a." Then it was as if long-frozen memories were melted and began to flow over him in waves. He thought of Hopi and Calm Sunset and the Man of Sorrows and his words and friendship. Finally he was able to speak of Ana's tragic death: "I cannot understand why this happened, but it's not fair to blame the Man of Sorrows." He had tried to pray a few times but quit; it all seemed so artificial. The few words he spoke were forced, and they felt hollow in his empty heart. There still was no joy.

Willie Juan felt nothing but self-hatred. Vanity and pride had blinded him; recognition, applause, and success had hardened his heart. His insensitivity to Ana shocked him. He had gained much, but lost much of what mattered most.

It was becoming dangerous for Willie Juan to be alone, and he knew it. Solitude can be fatal for a person, so he abruptly decided to leave Santa Fe to spend Christmas in Hopi with Calm Sunset.

The hardscrabble village of his youth had changed. The houses were now freshly painted, and there was electricity, winter heat, and bathtubs. Hopi now had a food bank, a farm co-op, and brand-new modern machinery to harvest the crops. The villagers expressed puzzlement over the mysterious benefactor who had paid for all of this. "Probably some rich industrialist from the north who is feeling guilty about all the people he cheated," they said.

As Willie Juan hobbled through the streets on his cane, he knew that the villagers had largely forgotten him. Their famous native son had uprooted himself from home. Surely they had figured he'd found greener pastures with wealthy gringos, and couldn't speak their language any longer. He couldn't blame their judgment of him. For the most part, they were right.

Yet Willie Juan was deeply hurt by their distance. He buried his feelings in small talk with his grandmother and in writing music. Calm Sunset was making two large piñatas for the children's Christmas celebration; Willie Juan could see enough to help her fill them with oranges and hard candy. He noticed that his grandmother could not speak to him without pain in her voice.

One morning a telegram arrived from Raphael Ramirez, the cardinal archbishop of Mexico City. Calm Sunset read the letter to Willie Juan,

Dear Willie Juan,

Your great gift to Hopi is recognized far and wide in Mexico. Now
that you are back in our country,
the people of God in Mexico would
be honored if you would share your
gift and play a trumpet medley at
the midnight Mass on Christmas Eve,
at the stadium in Mexico City.

Sincerely in Christ,
His Eminence,

Raphael Cardinal Ramirez

Willie Juan blinked in astonishment.

"You must do this. God is calling you," she said. Her voice, for the first time since his arrival, revealed delight.

"I wouldn't know what to play," said Willie Juan. "Christmas is a time of joy, and my heart is so sad. It is the birthday of Jesus, and I feel like I'm going to a funeral."

She put her hand on her grandson's shoulder. "Listen closely and play only what you hear in your heart."

When Willie Juan arrived at the concert hall, he could hear from backstage that the outdoor stadium was filled with what must have been a hundred thousand people. Cardinal Ramirez had told Willie Juan that men and women who never even went to church had flocked through the turnstiles. Even the president of Mexico was there with all of his political entourage. Willie Juan hoped that the peasants of Hopi had also taken their place in the bleachers.

Willie Juan knew that a 150-person cathedral choir stood

onstage, and he could hear the anxious foot-tapping of the philharmonic who sat in the orchestra pit.

The crowd quieted. Willie Juan heard the soft shuffle of the orchestra's maestro raising his baton, and a hundred thousand stadium voices broke into thunderous song with "O Come, All Ye Faithful." The Mass had begun. Willie Juan could feel the vibrations of the cardinal and his entourage entering in solemn procession.

The readings pierced Willie Juan's heart. He wept when the choir sang "Silent Night, Holy Night" as a responsorial song. During the homily the cardinal spoke softly and with deep emotion about Jesus, the child of Bethlehem, and the fullness of time. Still moved by "Silent Night, Holy Night," Willie Juan stood off in the wings, alone and lonely among the vast crowd. During the distribution of Communion, he continued waiting as the cathedral choir launched into the triumphant "Joy to the World." When everyone had returned to their seats, Cardinal Ramirez signaled for a quiet pause for meditation.

Cardinal Ramirez broke the silence with this simple introduction; he read a note from Calm Sunset: "Tonight we are privileged to be the first to hear a song written especially for this blessed occasion by a most gifted musician and composer, Willie Juan."

Somehow Willie Juan knew that his grandmother was smiling. Except for the choir and Calm Sunset, no one knew that Willie Juan had written a special song for the evening. He hadn't told a soul. He had performed his own music before, but this was the first time Willie Juan had ever written lyrics. The lyrics had come to him all at once, so quickly that Calm Sunset could hardly copy them down. But she did. And now it was time to share them.

Willie Juan stepped with his cane onto the podium, tears streaming down his cheeks. Then, in the beautiful afterglow of holy Communion, with the triumphant echo of "Joy to the World" still ringing, Willie Juan set down his cane, raised his horn, and blew a melody into the crisp, starlit winter night, as the choir sang:

> *Does anyone need me?*
> *Does anyone care?*
> *Does anyone love me?*
> *Is anyone there?*
>
> *I knew as a child*
> *The love of his eyes,*

But now as a man,
I believe nothing but lies.

I lost you, my friend,
the pain was too great.
I once knew of love,
but now only hate.

The vast audience gasped in stunned silence. Willie Juan's trumpet soared over the piano and rhythm section in long, achingly slow lines, lines that faded away into a wisp of music more imagined than heard.

Willie Juan heard the sound of people sobbing quietly as it spread through the stadium. He was playing his music for every one of them. He knew that many of those people, himself especially, had tried to tame their desires, reduce their longings, keep the pain at bay. Willie Juan's trumpet stared them all in the face, exposed their hearts, and pierced them to the quick. It did the same for Willie Juan.

Haunted by the memory of the Man of Sorrows, Willie Juan slowed his rhythm, as the choir continued his melody of longing:

Does anyone need me?
Does anyone care?
Does anyone love me?
Is anyone there?

You once showed your love
And said "I'll be your friend.
I'll never forsake you,
From now to the end."

Does anyone need me?
Does anyone care?
Does anyone love me?
Is anyone there?

Willie Juan became lost in his music and the choir members sang as if the night depended on them. Then suddenly, unnoticed by most of the crowd, someone from far out in the vast crowd began to blow his own horn. The sound raced to the stage like a train and Willie Juan lowered his trumpet.

At first he wasn't sure what he felt, then he knew; it was

recognition. He had felt this before, long ago, in the Cave of Bright Darkness. He knew who was playing that trumpet.

The song was a simple refrain, repeated over and over again, wave after wave of ... love. The sound enveloped the stadium. With unbearable intensity the man kept playing his horn. Miraculously the choir was able to put in words what the stranger played:

> *I'll always need you.*
> *I'll always care.*
> *Yes, I'll always love you.*
> *I'll always be there.*

It was as if scales had fallen from Willie Juan's eyes. Through the veil of his tears, he looked out and was shocked to see a light. Where there had only been darkness, now he saw traces of light. Willie Juan could sense something was approaching him, like a tree walking.

The tall, gaunt, angular great Man of Sorrows strode down the tear-drenched steps of the stadium with the peasants of Hopi gathered in dancing procession before him. As if moved by an irresistible force, the orchestra and choir broke into

Handel's "Messiah": "King of Kings and Lord of Lords, King of Kings and Lord of Lords."

He reached the elevated platform and raised his arms to each side, like the crucifix in the church. "Willie Juan," he said, "for many years the people have forgotten, they've fallen asleep. Tonight your pain and longing roused them, helped them to begin to remember something they lost along the way. Look out there, look around the stadium. See the faces of the men and women, aglow, alive. Your doubt-filled trust called them to life."

"O señor, I have wandered so far, gotten so lost, and I feel nothing inside. All I ever wanted, though I looked in the wrong places, was to find you. My life is so dark without you."

"Willie Juan, this is my birthday. You may ask for whatever you want and it's yours."

With the joy of a child at a fiesta, Willie Juan stammered, "Oh, my friend, you did not give up on me, even when I gave up on you. I dare not ask for anything more." But he could not help the image that flashed in his mind: his precious Ana Wim.

The Man of Sorrows looked deeply and tenderly into Willie Juan's eyes. "Merry Christmas, Little Brother. I want you to go home, Willie Juan. She will be waiting for you on the porch when you return to Hopi. Abba has raised Ana Wim from the dead and given her back to you as a living reminder of my presence, to help you not to forget. She will cry my tears, give you my hand, show you my heart, and hold you fast in my love. You will need each other, Willie Juan, as you walk hand in hand toward the house of Abba. I still have many things for the two of you to do."

Willie Juan stood in silence, wrapped in Abba's love. He managed to whisper: "Ana is alive?"

"Trust me. Now, will you do me a favor, my friend?"

"Anything," Willie Juan replied.

"Let's play together."

Willie Juan raised his horn in the shadow of the mighty Man of Sorrows. The two trumpets played "O Holy Night" in lyric duet as the hearts of men and women and children were stirred. As the final note hung in the night air, a child's whisper was heard: "Look, it's snowing."

night

"Go home, Willie Juan. She will be
waiting for you ... I still have many
things for the two of you to do."

Those words—perplexing and hopeful—echoed in Willie Juan's ears as the bus brakes hissed to a stop. Following the Christmas concert, he had quickly sold everything he had except his trumpet and a few remaining carvings, left his Santa Fe house in the hands of a realtor, and caught the first bus back to Hopi.

After the significant events surrounding the Christmas concert, the people of Hopi felt differently about Willie Juan. To show this change of heart, the mayor and people of Hopi had planned a grand homecoming party. But Willie Juan's bus was late due to mechanical problems. He finally arrived about midnight, after everyone had given up and gone to bed. He didn't mind; in fact he liked it that he was arriving home in the still of the night. There had been a lot of attention on him lately, and what he once had desired was now quite draining.

The bus driver pulled Willie Juan's bag from the storage area and then helped him carefully make his way down the steps of the bus. Even with the moments of vision at the concert, Willie Juan still lived in a world of mostly blindness. "Here you are, sir." As the bus pulled away, Willie Juan was left standing alone. The smell of mesquite filled his nose and brought tears to his still half-blind eyes. He had not realized how much he'd missed home.

Within minutes he heard the soft clop of hooves, probably a donkey's. As they grew closer, a voice spoke: "Willie Juan, the people wanted to welcome you home but it grew too late. I volunteered to stay and watch for your bus. I'll be happy to guide you home." Willie Juan felt he recognized the voice.

"Tino? Is that you?"

"Yes, Willie Juan. I wanted to be one of the first people to greet you. I heard you play in Mexico City at Christmas. It was beautiful. I want to apologize for the way I treated you when we were boys. I was so unkind to you. I'm so very sorry. Will you please forgive me?"

"Tino, I forgave you a long time ago. I can still remember, but it doesn't hurt me anymore.

"Thank you, Willie Juan. Thank you so much. Now let

me help you up in the wagon. I've got to get you home. She's awake, waiting for you."

"Thank you, Tino. Yes, I will be glad to see Calm Sunset."

"Calm Sunset went to sleep when everyone else did, Willie Juan. It's Ana who is waiting for you."

Willie Juan whispered within himself, "Ana?" Fear and wonder grabbed him. Could it really be true?

As Tino's wagon wheels creaked through the village, Willie Juan could hear someone humming. The sound grew stronger with each turn of the wheels. Finally, as the wagon stopped, the sound was a clear as the night, a beautiful melody from deep in Willie Juan's memory, unmistakable. It was Ana's song.

> *"Ave, ave, ave Ma-ri-a,*
> *Ave, ave, ave Mari-a ..."*

"Ana?" Willie Juan whispered.

Tino helped Willie Juan down, handed him his bag, and pointed his shoulders in the direction of the voice. "This is no childhood joke, my friend. Keep following the song, straight ahead. You're almost home."

As Willie Juan began to take his first step into a glass darkly, the humming stopped. Suddenly the song swept over him like afternoon rain. It was as if the song grew arms that hugged his neck and shed tears that wet his cheeks.

"Oh, Willie Juan! It's me, Ana!"

Willie Juan remembered that life-changing day when he'd truly seen her face on the street corner: brown eyes, perky nose, radiant countenance. But that was when his vision was good; could he really trust what poor vision he had left? Ana had been hit by a car and killed—was this *really* her? Was she *really* alive?

He then felt two soft hands take his face, two soft lips kiss his forehead, and then a single whisper in his ear: "Willie Juanito, it's *really* me!"

No one had ever called him Willie Juanito … except Ana.

Willie Juan remembered a line from a novel: "Only God knows how much I love you." It was exactly the way he felt about Ana. The days and weeks that followed for Willie Juan could only be described as *loca d'amor*—"crazed with love."

One March evening, as they walked along the banks of the Rio Grande, Willie Juan was filled with courage as doves cooed the dusk. He paused and asked a question he'd asked once before: "Ana, I love you with all my heart. Will you marry me?" Ana answered: "Oh, Willie Juanito! I'd love to." There was no hesitation in her voice. And that was that.

The village of Hopi now turned all their attention to the upcoming wedding of Willie Juan and Ana Wim. The date was set—Easter Sunday. Gone were the hardscrabble shacks and crumbling adobe buildings of Willie Juan's childhood. His generous donations to the village resulted in lovely, small adobe houses surrounded by beautifully cobbled pathways that all led to the church in the center of the village. Here, in the middle of everything, beneath the crucifix that held the Man of Sorrows, is where Willie Juan and Ana Wim would be married.

As the holy days approached, the week before Easter, Calm Sunset told Willie Juan that she would prepare a special dinner on Thursday evening, Maundy Thursday, for him and Ana. After a wonderful meal of juicy fajitas, savory corn bread, Raggedy Ann pudding, and sweet potato pie, Calm Sunset got up from the table and knelt at Willie Juan and

Ana's feet. "Little ones, I want to wash your feet this night." Willie Juan began to protest, but then reconsidered. He had learned by this point in his life that gifts are to be received, enjoyed. Calm Sunset proceeded to wash their dusty feet. She then turned to Ana.

"Ana, I have two gifts for you. First, I want you to have this aloe plant. I used it to soothe the wounds I could see on Willie Juan when he was a child. Second, I want you to have my rocking chair. I used it to ease the wounds I could not see, but knew were there. I believe you will be a blessing to many children and these gifts will serve you well. I love you, Ana Wim. You are truly a gift from God."

Willie Juan watched as she shifted on old knees, turning to speak directly to her grandson. "Willie Juan, my gift to you is in the form of a request. It may sound strange to you now, but if you'll trust me, I believe you'll one day understand. I am old now. Someday soon, Willie Juan, you'll know when, I want you to make one last journey to the Cave of Bright Darkness. It will be difficult enough with your eyesight so weak and your body will be old and brittle by then, but that is my gift to you, strange as it may seem. Only God knows how much I love you, Willie Juan. You are truly a gift from God."

Easter Sunday morning dawned bright and fresh. Tino helped Willie Juan adjust his bolo tie, while several of the other men in the village placed clean blankets in the back of Tino's wagon. Willie Juan sat on the edge of the wagon, waiting. As Ana Wim emerged from the adobe, it was as if heaven itself gasped. She was wearing the redolent ocotillo flowers in her hair; the smell filled Willie Juan's senses. Ana sat beside him on the back of the wagon and took his hand. Tino's wagon began its journey down the cobbled streets toward the church. As the village children walked beside the wagon, their voices filled the air. Father Thomas had recently taught them the French Easter cry: "*L'amour de Dieu est folie*"—the love of God is folly … the love of God is folly.

Calm Sunset watched from her doorstep as they inched away. Just moments before, Willie Juan had asked her with a grin: "Any last word?"

"Willie Juan, just know that to live in this world you have to love flesh and blood, hold it close, know when to let go, and then let go."

"That's more than one word, Grandmother." And with that he hugged her tightly. And then let go.

The entire village came out for the wedding. Father Thomas had come to the church in Hopi only six months ago, but the people quickly accepted him. The rumor was that his rather unorthodox liturgies got him kicked out of one of the larger churches.

"Willie Juan and Ana, Abba is very fond of you. Remember this moment. After today you shall say to the world—This is my husband. This is my wife.

"Do you promise to love each other?"

Willie Juan looked at Ana through near-blind eyes and said, "Yes. I do."

Ana whispered, "I do too."

Never before had applause erupted in the little village church. It even took Father Thomas by surprise. Willie Juan and Ana turned and faced the people. The large crucifix cast an almighty shadow down the middle aisle. The new couple stepped into it and the rest of their lives.

In the years that followed, Willie Juan and Ana found they would not be able to have children. After Calm Sunset's gifts of the aloe and rocking chair to Ana, Willie Juan found it hard to understand. Why would Abba deny their wish for a child? The question left him bitter. He was not proud of it, but the bitterness was there nonetheless.

Ana took to making sopapillas around dusk. And humming. She would retrieve the pastries from the oil when golden, dust them with sugar, and then open the back door. Between her humming and the delicious smell of the sopapillas, children and animals showed up each evening. Ana would pass fresh honey around so the children could fill the hollow dough. The sweetness of children's laughter and the wagging tails of dogs seemed to fill the hollow in Ana.

Father Thomas showed up one evening about the time the first batch of sopapillas came out of the oil. "Might there be one for an old kid?" he said with a smile.

Ana kept humming, a smile coming through her voice, and handed him the honey. Willie Juan could hear their interactions from his rocking chair across the patio.

"I actually came by to see Willie Juan," Father Thomas said. "Is he here?" At that Willie Juan called for the father to join him. When Father Thomas stepped into the room, Willie Juan patted the chair beside him. "Have a seat."

"Willie Juan, I'm not much on instruction, you know that," Father Thomas began. "Besides, you've had some Abba experiences that most of us only dream of having. But I do try and remind people of things they might have forgotten. Anyone can sing in the light, but it's those who can whisper a doxology in darkness who are truly grateful. Hey, that's not bad. I should write that down."

Willie Juan smiled. Father Thomas stood and headed back for another sopapilla. "You've got a house full of children, Willie Juan. It just doesn't look like you thought it would."

And with that thought, Willie Juan remembered the Medicine Man's words: "Go home, Willie Juan. She will be waiting for you on the porch when you return to Hopi. Abba has raised Ana Wim from the dead and given her back to you as a living reminder of my presence … I still have many things for the two of you to do." And for the first time in weeks, Willie Juan chuckled, mainly at himself. "Ana has always cared for the least of these. It was one of the qualities I first found most attractive about her. That is her gift, our gift, to the village.

How could I have been so *blind*?" After a second's pause the two men laughed like boys.

Just then Willie Juan felt a hand take his. The fingers were small, those of a child, most likely a little boy. "Mr. Willie Juan, Ana needs your help. She asked me to lead you back."

"And what is your name, little one?" Willie Juan asked.

"My name is John."

And so, most evenings, in the middle of their years, the home of Willie Juan and Ana Wim was filled with children. They loved all the children equally but also loved them differently. Ana taught many of them to make sopapillas, so well that one summer evening the children did all the cooking. As they sat around eating the pastries, Willie Juan asked the children, "When you get to heaven, little friends, do you know what Abba will ask you?" One little girl said, "He'll say, 'Were you a good girl?'" Another boy piped up and said, "No, he'll ask how many prayers we prayed." One small red-headed girl said she was afraid of Abba. Willie

Juan tried to calm her fears: "Oh, little one, there's no need to be afraid of Abba. Listen closely and I'll tell you Abba's question." The children stopped eating and held their breath. "Abba will ask, 'Did you enjoy the sopapilla?'" The children laughed in unison, and Willie Juan joined in with a giggle. Then he continued. "Abba wants you to live with gratitude, enjoying his gifts." After a little more discussion, the children all returned to the sopapillas, everyone, that is, except John.

Ever since he'd led Willie Juan to the kitchen that evening months ago, John stayed in Willie Juan's shadow. Or maybe it was Willie Juan who stayed in John's shadow. One night Ana mentioned his sidekick. Willie Juan said, "Yes, I think he wants to make sure I don't miss anything. One afternoon he pointed out a raven and then one evening, about dusk, he drew my attention to a coyote."

After the children returned to eating their sopapillas, John approached Willie Juan with pastry in hand. "Mr. Willie Juan, would you like to share my sopapilla with me?" The question stunned Willie Juan; all he could think of was the day the Medicine Man had asked a similar question. He remembered that on that day his heart even beat differently. Willie Juan had the same feeling after John's question.

"Yes, I would like to share your sopapilla." Willie Juan
then looked toward John's face. "J-John ... would you be my
friend?"

"Mr. Willie Juan, I am your friend."

Father Thomas asked Willie Juan to fill in for him one
Sunday at the adobe church in the center of the village. "My
favorite aunt died, Willie Juan, and I need to travel and
attend her funeral service. She was the one who first told me
of Abba's love." His words reminded Willie Juan of Calm
Sunset and the ways she would rock him and whisper of
Abba's mercy. Calm Sunset had died several years ago. Willie
Juan remembered her final words: "It's not a tragedy when
someone dies at the end of her life."

"All right, Thomas. Yes, I'll help you out. But I'm not sure
what I'll say. I'm getting older."

Father Thomas said, "We all are, Willie Juan. I'm sure you'll
think of something. You'll do fine, don't worry."

Word spread in the village that Willie Juan would be speaking the next Sunday at church. Everyone planned to be there. It had been years since the wedding of Willie Juan and Ana. Although he and Ana were there each Sunday among the people, that was the last time he had stood before the people in the village church.

Over breakfast one morning Ana could tell Willie Juan was preoccupied with Father Thomas's invitation. She asked, "Do you know what you're going to say to the people?"

"I think I'll tell them what it means to be a friend: You don't have to understand your friends, just love them. What do you think?" asked Willie Juan.

"I think I love you, Willie Juanito. You'll do fine, don't worry. Now eat or …"

"Or what?" Willie Juan grinned.

"Or I'll tell all the village your socks have holes in them and you won't let me mend them." Ana waited for his response. He knew it was as she expected. He just laughed, then started eating.

The adobe walls of the church swelled with people. The air smelled of autumn, crisp, full of change. The village children sang a song to begin the service:

> *Oh, he called the little children, and sat 'em on his knee;*
> *glory, sing to the Lord.*
> *Then he hugged 'em and caressed 'em, till they didn't want to*
>   *leave him;*
> *glory, sing to the Lord.*

As the children made way their way back to their seats, John, now almost twelve, stood beside the pew where Willie Juan sat. "I'll lead you up the steps, Mr. Willie Juan."

As Willie Juan faced the people, it was as if the darkness in his eyes also moved across his thoughts. He could not remember what he had planned to say. In fact he could not think of anything to say, anything at all. The people sat, hushed. The seconds that passed felt like hours to Willie Juan. Finally Ana made her way up beside Willie Juan and took his trembling hands. "Come now, my love. My lovely one, come."

Ana and Willie Juan slowly walked down the middle aisle

of the adobe church. The people of the village of Hopi stood, row by row, as their friends passed by.

Willie Juan grew listless, dreaming of the past: Calm Sunset, the Medicine Man, and the Cave of Bright Darkness. His mind and body were weary. He remembered old men and women in the village using the phrase "when the river calls your name." He now knew what they meant. He could hear it. Willie Juan knew that Ana could see what was happening.

One day Willie Juan overheard Ana speaking to John. "John, I need your help."

"Whatever I can do, Ana. You know that." Their voices grew hushed so he couldn't quite make out what Ana said next, but he heard John's reply: "Are you certain I'm the one?"

"Yes, John," Ana said with resolve." He trusts you."

The following Thursday found the people of the village of Hopi busy with final preparations for the Fiesta of the Virgin of the Assumption. It was still an occasion of great celebration along the Rio Grande. Nevertheless most of the villagers found time to pass by Willie Juan's adobe and wave or speak or sit if only for a moment. The day held a clarity for Willie Juan; he remembered names and told stories. There were days for Willie Juan when the infinitely tender hand of Abba seemed to briefly hold the darkness at bay. This was such a day, a good day.

Father Thomas was the final visitor that evening. He sat on the back porch with Willie Juan and Ana. They drank black coffee and ate sopapillas filled with honey and let the birds do the talking. It was Communion, Willie Juan realized. A good ending to a good day.

The next morning Ana walked Willie Juan out to the wagon. There, Willie Juan realized that John had been waiting for him. It was early; the day was still just waking up. Ana handed John a basket of food for the trip: enchiladas stuffed with chicken, savory corn bread, sweet potato pie, and, of course, sopapillas and honey. John placed the basket in the back of the buckboard, rearranging the blankets and water he'd brought along, before returning to the driver's seat. Ana turned Willie Juan to face her.

"My Willie Juanito. Do you remember that Calm Sunset wanted you to return to the Cave of Bright Darkness one last time?"

Willie Juan remembered.

"John will guide you there," Ana continued. "He will take you as far as he can, but you'll have to take the last steps yourself. Don't be afraid. The question for your life has always been 'Will you trust?' You are being asked once again, Willie Juanito. Don't worry; all will be well."

Willie Juan was moved by his wife's tenderness. "Life really is a gift, isn't it?" Willie Juan whispered.

"Yes, my love, it really is."

Ana kissed his cheek, rubbed her thumbs through his eyebrows, and draped a thin quilt around his shoulders.

"What's this?" Willie Juan asked.

"It's the patchwork quilt Calm Sunset was working on before she died. I believe she would want you to have it for this trip. I do too." Ana then helped him up in the wagon. John eased the reins just enough that the two mules started walking. Willie Juan turned and waved. He could not see Ana, but he knew she was there.

The two pilgrims reached the approach by mid-morning. John took the wagon in as far as he could; from now on their journey would be on foot. With one hand on a cane and the other around John's neck, Willie Juan began the final ascent to the rim.

"John, you may regret your decision to help me. I'm old and slow."

"Willie Juan, let's take a few steps, catch our breath, and then a few steps more. One foot in front of the other."

So they began their step-pause, step-pause approach up the steep ascent. The sun was almost overhead by now; the men were sweating through their shirts. Willie Juan stumbled and fell twice, the second time taking John down with him. As they sat with scraped elbows and palms, Willie Juan began to giggle. Then his giggle turned into a belly laugh, infectious enough to get John laughing as well.

And then a memory surfaced, one Willie Juan had almost forgotten. "John, did I ever tell you about the time a classmate dared me to climb this ridge?"

"No. I'd love to hear it. But why don't you tell me as we walk? Just a little farther and we can gain some shade. Deal?"

And so Willie Juan told the story of Antonio, which led to the story of the Medicine Man, which led to the story of the amorine, which led to the story of his experience in the Cave of Bright Darkness. Willie Juan's mind had seemed cloudy back in the village, but now he seemed sharp, crisp. Just as beneficial, the telling of his story took their minds off the difficult ascent, until suddenly they looked up and there was the stone staircase leading down to the cave. A rock overhang provided a pleasant shade, so they took a much-needed break and ate some enchiladas and sopapillas.

"John, are you enjoying what you're eating right now?"

"Yes, Willie Juan. Everything is delicious."

"Good. It is important to Abba's heart that we enjoy the gifts he gives. There are twenty-eight steps down from here, what Calm Sunset called the 'dazzling darkness of sheer trust' and then we reach the cave. I'm ready when you are."

"Do we ever really trust when we can see, Willie Juan?"

"I'd love to tell you otherwise, John, but what faith I have has been strengthened in the dark. It's just the way it is."

"I was afraid you were going to say that. All right, I'm ready, let's go."

As they reached the parapet before the entrance to the cave, Willie Juan stopped and steadied himself.

"John, we must stay until one hour after sunset. Just sit with me, calmly and patiently. Listen to the silence. Have courage. Courage is like becoming friends with what lies around the corner. And John, when you return, take care of Ana."

As they entered the cave, they immediately felt the cool on their skin. They saw a stone slab about halfway back, covered in burlap bags. In one corner, there was a kerosene lamp, a rickety chair, and a battered oak table. The other corner held a stone altar; a tall crucifix stood behind it. Willie Juan pointed to the stone slab and John led him there. John sat on the floor next to the slab while Willie Juan clambered up on top. In no time Willie Juan was fast asleep.

Willie Juan's sleep was interrupted by the sound of footsteps on the stone stairwell growing closer to the entrance to the cave. He remained quiet as he watched through his near-blindness a tall, gaunt man walk through the entrance.

"The Man of Sorrows," John said fearlessly. "Willie Juan

told me all about you. Ana asked me to help him return here once more. But I don't know what to do now."

The Medicine Man approached John and sat down beside him. "Thank you, John. It is not a slight thing to help those who are so very young or so very old. You've done well. John, do you know what your name means?"

"Yes, it means 'beloved.'"

Willie Juan smiled as he lay still. He had taught John the meaning of his name when they had first become friends some years ago.

"That's right. I have a challenge for you. Would you like to hear it?"

"Yes," John said.

"Go back and live out your name; live like the beloved of Abba. Some may ask you, but most others will simply observe the way you live. Some will call you crazy, some may even try and silence your voice, but some will stop and wonder. Your courage in living as Abba's beloved can give others the strength to do the same. For in the end only one thing remains—Abba's love. Willie Juan has known that, but the river is calling his name. John, now it is your turn: Define yourself as one beloved by God."

Willie Juan, no longer able to stay still with the Man of Sorrows present, stood and stretched his limbs and walked directly over to where the Medicine Man and John sat, smiling all the way.

"Hello, Little Brother," the Medicine Man said with a smile that Willie Juan could make out clearly. The Medicine Man stood and embraced Willie Juan.

Willie Juan took him by the shoulders. "Oh, señor, it is so good to see you." Willie Juan turned his gaze toward John. "Friend, I see you've met the Medicine Man I told you about."

"Yes, we've met … Mr. Willie Juan, can you see?"

"I'm beginning to, John. I'm beginning to."

The Medicine Man extended a hand to John and then raised him up. "You'd best be on your way, my friend. Remember, only one thing remains."

Willie Juan squeezed John's shoulder. "You know the way home. Thank you, John. And don't forget to watch out for Ana."

Willie Juan and the Medicine Man began telling each other stories and laughing as John made his way up the stone stairwell. "You will be with him, Medicine Man?" Willie Juan asked.

"Yes, Willie Juan, like I've always been with you."

The men of sorrows walked to the edge of the cave and watched John fade into the night.

"It's time to go, Willie Juan."

"Yes, I know."

Willie Juan could just make out the lights of the village of Hopi in the distance as he walked with the Medicine Man along the rim. It was the first day of the Fiesta of the Virgin of the Assumption. A good day. A very good day.

keep reading for a sample of ...

brennan manning

the furious longing of God

intro

I'm Brennan. I'm an alcoholic.

How I got there, why I left there, why I went back, is the
story of my life.

But it is not the whole story.

I'm Brennan. I'm a Catholic.

How I got there, why I left there, why I went back, is also the
story of my life.

But it is not the whole story.

I'm Brennan. I was a priest, but am no longer a priest. I was a
married man but am no longer a married man.

How I got to those places, why I left those places, is the story
  of my life too.
But it is not the whole story.

I'm Brennan. I'm a sinner, saved by grace.
That is the larger and more important story.
Only God, in His fury, knows the whole of it.

For two years, between 1971 and 1973, I lived with a community
of Franciscans in Bayou La Batre, Alabama. Three were priests,
two were lay brothers. I was thirty-five years old at the time, the
adventure of my faith in full sail. The shore was a port city, the second largest in the United States, after the one in New York.

   A few of us worked on the shrimp boats there whenever
they needed help. It was short-term work, ten days at sea,

trawling for shrimp, flounder, snapper. We were always careful when we went to sea. Always.

One day we were on our way home from Beaumont when we caught the end of a Texas tailstorm. The water was calm at first. And our forty-five-foot-long boat bobbed lazily in the water like the boat on the cover of this book. But suddenly the clouds gathered and the temperature dropped. The sea began to churn, sweeping spray across the bow. Waves pummeled the sides of the boat. Our seasoned captain told us to get below. Below deck, we reached for metal handles and dear life.

I was convinced we were going to die.

Then the storm, the real storm, hit. Winds of 120 miles per hour. Sudden swells ten feet high. It was a fury unleashed.

Someone once said, *If a man would learn to pray, let him go to sea.*

My life has been a life lived in God's furious longing. And I have learned to pray.

genesis

The genesis of this book originated in 1978 during a thirty-day silent, directed retreat at a spiritual center in Wernersville, Pennsylvania. My director, a Jesuit priest named Bob Hamm, guided me to a passage in the Song of Solomon:

I AM MY BELOVED'S,

AND HIS DESIRE IS FOR ME.

(7:10 NASB)

This is the passage I prayed for the duration of my time there.

Over the past thirty years, I have prayed that passage (Song of Solomon 7:10ff.) in soaring 747s, monasteries, caves, retreat centers, and deserted places. I believe His desire for you and me can best be described as a *furious longing*. If you don't get anything else out of this book, I hope you begin to pray that passage. When you take those words personally, I mean very personally, a number of beautiful things come to pass:

- The drumbeats of doom in your head will be replaced by a song in your heart, which could lead to a twinkle in your eye.
- You will not be dependent on the company of others to ease your loneliness, for He is Emmanuel—God with us.
- The praise of others will not send your spirit soaring, nor will their criticism plunge you into the pit. Their rejection may make you sick, but it will not be a sickness unto death.
- In a significant interior development, you will move from I *should* pray to I *must* pray.
- You will live with an awareness that the Father not only loves you, but likes you.

- You will stop comparing yourself with others. In the same way, you will not trumpet your own importance, boast about your victories in the vineyard, or feel superior to anyone.
- You will read Zephaniah 3:17–18 and see God dancing for joy because of you (the *Jerusalem Bible* translation is accurate).
- Off and on throughout the day, you will just know that you are being seen by Jesus with a gaze of infinite tenderness.

I am a witness to these truths.

There is no need to mince words. I believe that Christianity happens when men and women experience the reckless, raging confidence that comes from knowing the God of Jesus Christ. I've said that before in books and talks, and it'd be blasphemous for that not to show up here at the beginning of this book.

In my forty-four years of ministry, the furious love of God has been the dominant theme of my life. I've varied with titles such as *Ragamuffin Gospel*, *Abba's Child*, and *The Relentless Tenderness of Jesus*, but they are all facets of the same gem: that the shattering truth of the transcendent God seeking intimacy with us is not well served by gauzy sentimentality, schmaltz, or a naked appeal to emotion, but rather in the boiling bouillabaisse of shock bordering on disbelief, wonder akin to incredulity, and affectionate awe tinged by doubt.

The furious longing of God is beyond our wildest desires, our hope or hopelessness, our rectitude or wickedness, neither cornered by sweet talk nor gentle persuasion. The furious longing of God, as Dan Berrigan writes, is "not to be reduced to a thing, a grand ideal; it is not to be reduced to a plaything, a caged songbird, for the amusement of children." It cannot be tamed, boxed, captivated, housebroken, or templebroken. It is simply and startlingly Jesus, the effulgence of the Father's love.

The seldom-stated truth is that many of us have a longing for God and an aversion to God. Some of us seek Him and flee Him at the same time. We may scrupulously observe the Ten Commandments and rarely miss church on a Sunday morning, but a love affair with Jesus is just not our cup of tea.

I don't really think that about you. If that were the case, you wouldn't have searched the couch cushions for change to buy this book. I am writing *The Furious Longing of God* truthfully and candidly, to share of the God who has revealed Himself in my personal history. After you've read it, I hope you'll drop it at a used bookstore where some ragamuffin will pick it up and she'll say, "Cool." Then maybe she'll pass it on to some poor wretch who is bedraggled, beat up, and burned out, and he'll shout, "Wow!"

I am witness to the truth that Abba still whispers:

COME THEN, MY BELOVED,

MY LOVELY ONE, COME.

FOR SEE, WINTER IS PAST,

THE RAINS ARE OVER AND GONE.

FLOWERS ARE APPEARING ON THE EARTH. THE

SEASON OF GLAD SONGS HAS COME,

THE COOING OF THE TURTLEDOVE
IS HEARD IN OUR LAND.

THE FIG TREE IS FORMING ITS FIRST FIGS AND THE
BLOSSOMING VINES GIVE OUT THEIR FRAGRANCE.

COME THEN, MY BELOVED, MY LOVELY
ONE, COME. (SONG 2:10–13 NJB)

CONSIDER THIS...

1. When you read that phrase—the furious longing of God—what emotions or images does it evoke?

2. "... I *should* pray to I *must* pray." How would you describe the difference between the two?

about the author

Brennan Manning has spent the past forty years helping others experience the reality of God's love and grace. It's at the heart of everything he's written and done. A recovering alcoholic and former Franciscan priest, his spiritual journey has taken him down a variety of paths. He has taught seminarians, spoken to packed arenas, lived in a cave and labored with the poor in Spain, and ministered to shrimpers in Alabama. Brennan is best known as the author of the contemporary classics *The Ragamuffin Gospel*, *Abba's Child*, *Ruthless Trust*, and *The Importance of Being Foolish*.

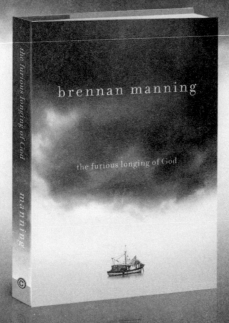